Weddings

& Courtships

Ireland

Love and Romance

The Irish Way

Lisa Shea

Print version ISBN 978-1500196837

ASIN: B00UR53VOA

Visit WeddingsAndCourtships.com for more details about this series.

This is the fully updated front-to-back revised 2015 version of the book I first wrote in 2002.

Contents

Weddings

& Courtships

Ireland

Introduction

"When Irish eyes are smiling,
Sure, 'tis like the morn in Spring.
In the lilt of Irish laughter
You can hear the angels sing.
When Irish hearts are happy,
All the world seems bright and gay.
And when Irish eyes are smiling,
Sure, they steal your heart away."

—Chauncey Olcott, 1912

Ah, Ireland! The land of heartfelt romance. Every time I go to Ireland I'm reminded of why I love it so – and every time I leave I start planning when I can return again. Ireland exudes romance from its cozy taverns to its windswept ocean walks, from its thatch-roofed cottages to its rolling fields of green.

Irish friendship is found in the enthusiastic dancing and boisterous song filling a warm pub on a rainy evening. An Irish home is a place of fertile fields lined with stone walls and filled with beautiful wildflowers. Ireland is a land of craftsmen and talented artists. Ireland's poets are world renowned. Irish musicians please audiences of all backgrounds. Waterford crystal and Aran sweaters are sought after in every corner of the world.

Every St. Patrick's Day, millions of people look back through their lineage for their Irish roots or lay claim to honorary Irish blood. Whatever their background, they toast to luck with an Irish brew. For such a small island (under 33,000 square miles total) the love and affection that Ireland engenders reaches from the United States to Australia and all points in between.

One of the most enduring images that Ireland elicits is one of love and romance. There is the old Irish couple, walking hand in hand down a hedge-lined lane, content with each other after decades of happy marriage. There is the young Irish girl, weaving wildflowers into her hair, dreaming of her true love. There is the Irish lad heading off to sea to make his fortune in America, promising to come back to the girl he adores when he has earned enough money to be worthy of her.

It can be easy to bring the magic of Irish love and romance into your own life! This book will cover it all, so that no matter what stage of life you're in, you'll find something to inspire you. Read it again in a few years and you'll discover that an entirely different section now sparks fresh spring into your step. From movies to music, from travel ideas to home decorating, there's something for everyone when it comes to wearing the green.

Sláinte—Cheers!

Note for those who buy this book in its in black-and-white paperback version: The purchase of the paperback copy grants you FREE access to the full-color Kindle version. Even if you don't own a Kindle, you can still read the book on your PC or Mac. This means all the beautiful photos can be seen in full color. It's worth taking a look! Most of these were taken by me and Bob on our trips.

Irish Legends and Lore

"Oh, list to the lay of a poor Irish harper
And scorn not the strains of his old withered hand
But remember his fingers they once could move sharper
To raise up the memory of his dear native land."
—The Bard of Armagh, traditional

Ireland has a long history stretching back into the mists of pre-Christianity. There were humans on this beautiful, green island as far back as 8,000BC. The fantastic tomb of Newgrange was built in 3,200BC. In comparison, the Giza Pyramid was built nearly a thousand years later.

Living on Ireland was a challenge, with invaders coming in from all sides as well as inter-clan fighting. The legends of Ireland involve love and romance, of strong Irish men with their able wives by their sides. In the mists of the past, Irish men were strong and sure, ready with a laugh, and capable of defending their homes from all dangers.

Irish women were treasured for their strength, their wit, and their passion. An Irish woman was not frail and fragile. She would not break if handled roughly. In times of trouble, she would be right beside her mate, fiercely protecting her family and household. With those she loved, her tenderness was warm and dependable.

Irish boys and girls grew up steeped in these traditions. The centuries-old folk stories were shared by the family at night, and references to the stories came up easily in conversation. Ireland is a land of storytellers and eager audiences, from the youngest tyke to the oldest pensioner.

In western culture, young lovers with families who disapproved might think immediately of Romeo and Juliet. A young girl whose sisters always seemed to get preferential treatment might dream of Cinderella and of her prince. The traditional Irish legends affected the Irish in the same manner, giving Irish couples something to relate to and to dream of.

Read on to learn more about the some of the most popular tales of Ireland. This is but a brief look into a culture which has a long tradition of heroes and heroines. It's well worth it to get a book or two on Irish folklore and immerse yourself into these tales. They give strong insight into what makes the Irish culture so special.

Conchobar mac Nessa

The tales of Conchobar mac Nessa are set in the centuries just after Christ, and are part of the "Ulster Cycle" of stories in Ireland. In Ireland, they don't just have single stories like "the tale of Paul Revere's Ride." They have incredibly complicated, interwoven epics made up of large casts of characters engaged in bloody war, passionate affairs, deceptions, and betrayals. Think of it as a Game of Thrones sequence being told around hearth-fires in the evening for entertainment. The whole family would listen in, enraptured by the tales and storylines.

In the days of old there was a High King who ruled over all the lands, and then lower kings which controlled each county. One of those counties was County Ulster.

Key to the Ulster Cycle was Conchobar mac Nessa. He was fortunate to be born to an intelligent, strategically-thinking mother. When Conchobar was only seven, his mom married the King of Ulster and asked if her son could temporarily be king for a year. The king thought this over and agreed, figuring it was a way to please his new wife without any real harm. After all, what could a seven year old do?

Sure enough, Conchobar and his mom were such stunning rulers that when the year was up everyone demanded that they stay in power. A battle ensued and when the dust settled, Conchobar was given the hand of the High King's daughter to seal his relationship with that family.

Just as with most epics, Conchobar's life was not meant to be easy. The first daughter he wed, Medb, was hostile. She ended up leaving him. He then wed Eithne, another daughter of the High King. Eithne has multiple meanings – both "little fire" and "sweet kernel of a nut." So she was both tender and passionate – the perfect combination in most Irish tales. However, life in these tales is rarely easy. Medb is jealous of how well Conchobar and Eithne are getting along and drowns her.

Conchobar moves along to sister number three, Mugain, but again he is unlucky. She fell in love with the court poet and had an affair.

Then Conchobar hears a prophecy that an infant girl will grow up to be a great beauty. He decides to raise her, kept away from all other men, and then marry her when she comes of age. Unfortunately for Conchobar, she ends up seeing another young warrior her own age and runs off with him.

What do these tales tell us about Ireland? The Irish expect life and love to be challenging. There will be ups and downs. Life rarely goes smoothly. Still, if you keep your wits about you, stay ready for love, and be willing to pursue it when the opportunity arises, sometimes you can grab that moment in the sun.

Queen Medb and Ailill

Queen Medb is one of the most famous women in Irish history, and indeed in much of Western History. She was a woman who was beautiful, intelligent, a great warrior, and a military strategist. In pre-Christian Ireland it was usual to take lovers and to separate when a marriage no longer brought fulfillment. Medb enjoyed having lovers. She divorced two men when they could no longer keep up with her on the field or in discussions. One was Conchobar mac Nessa, who we just heard about. The next was the King of Connacht, Tinni mac Conri. She had an affair with her bodyguard, Ailill. When Tinni found out he challenged Ailill to single combat, lost, and now Ailill became Medb's husband and king.

Medb was thrilled. Ailill and Medb were both great warriors, intelligent speakers, and equally rich. Their passion for one other was legendary. There was only one stone in Maeve's shoe - Ailill owned a gorgeous white bull named "Finnbernach." As marriages could easily come and go in those days, careful attention was paid to who owned what, so when the two parted ways each could leave with what they brought. Medb was a strong and proud woman and was in all ways an equal to her husband. The two were playfully competitive, each prodding the other to greater feats and tasks. When Ailill became renowned for his gorgeous bull, Maeve wished to have one as well. Eager to match her husband's holdings, Medb became obsessed with a brown bull with which she could equal her husband's wealth.

Medb sent her retainers to buy the brown bull, and the owners gladly accepted. However, during the feasting which followed the agreement, the retainers got drunk. They boasted that they could easily have taken the bull by force had they wished to. Upset, the owners took back their acceptance of the terms. They told the retainers that Medb could go ahead and try to take the bull, if she felt she could. On hearing this, Medb accepted the challenge, gathered her troops and set forth to steal the bull.

This was the famous "Cattle Raid of Cooley."

CúChulainn, the great warrior, stood in Maeve's way, defending Ulster and the owner of the bull. Maeve sent hero after hero against CúChulainn to no effect. Her warriors did finally defeat him, and returned triumphantly back home with her prize.

Ironically, Maeve's new brown bull would not share the pasture with the white bull. The two fought, and both died. Thus were Maeve and Ailill again fully equal in their relationship, and members of an epic tale which lives even to today.

Again we see in this story just how much the Irish treasured strength in both men and women. Medb was craved by many men for her passion and talents. She wasn't expected to be a quiet mouse sitting in a corner. She could lead troops, plan attacks, and run a household as well.

CúChulainn and Emer

Who was this great hero, CúChulainn, who stood so boldly against Medb and her cattle-rustling ambitions?

CúChulainn was the son of King Conchobar's sister. CúChulainn grew up a beloved member in King Conchobar's court. The young boy was respected throughout the land for his bravery and strength. He was only a teenager when he held off the waves of attackers that Queen Medb sent to steal the bull.

There were many stories told about CúChulainn's bravery. Where the tales in the Ulster stories about King Conchobar and Queen Medb often involve betrayal, wild emotions, and tragic ends, CúChulainn was more of a King Arthur figure. He stood for dependability. He was the one warrior who could be relied on to stand his ground and do what was right.

For example, in one tale, Queen Medb's husband, King Ailill, was asked to determine the greatest warrior in Ireland. CúChulainn and two other contenders were put in a room overnight. Monsters were sent in, and while the two other warriors hid in the rafters, CúChulainn faced his monsters. In the morning, despite the evidence of their cowardice, the other two warriors claimed the contest was unfair.

King Ailill created another contest for them. He set giants in against the three warriors. Again, CúChulainn was the only one to emerge victorious, but the other two disagreed.

Finally, while the group is pondering what to do next, a giant entered and offered to lay his head down on a chopping block and have his head removed, if only the hero would then agree to do the same the following night. If a champion was not found to do this, he would lay waste to the land. The other two champions immediately offered to these terms. One of them chopped off the giant's head. However, the giant returned the following evening, and the champion was nowhere to be found. The second champion then chopped off the giant's head, but was also missing when his own turn came.

Finally CúChulainn stepped up and removed the giant's head. CúChulainn then dutifully sat and waited. When the giant returned, CúChulainn laid his own head on the block. The giant revealed that he was Curoi of Kerry, a wise man. He praised CúChulainn for defending his land with his own life, then proclaimed CúChulainn as the wise and just champion of the land.

The other soldiers at King Conor's court became jealous of CúChulainn and made an effort to find a suitable wife for him, so that he would be less tempting to their own wives and daughters. After a year of looking, not one girl was found that was felt to be worthy. CúChulainn decided to take a look for himself. He headed out to find a woman he'd heard of named Emer, who was said to be both intelligent and beautiful.

When CúChulainn rode up to Emer's home, Emer was sitting with her sister and other village women, teaching them how to sew. She looked up to see CúChulainn there, and asked him what he wanted. He knew that she was smart, and answered in a way that showed his interest in her without revealing it to the others. Soon the pair found they were well matched for each other. Emer told him that only the greatest of warriors would be able to claim her, and he agreed to her challenges. Unfortunately for the pair, Emer's father hated CúChulainn and vowed to put a stop to the courtship when he found out about it.

Emer's father went to CúChulainn in disguise and convinced him that he should go train in battle in Scotland with a famous female warrior. His hope was that CúChulainn would be killed in a war there and never return. Emer realized what was happening and warned CúChulainn to take care.

CúChulainn trained for a year, and then fought bravely to prove his worthiness to Emer. When he returned to her, her father still forbade them to marry, now claiming the elder sister had to marry first. Emer's father then challenged CúChulainn and sent warriors to kill him. CúChulainn defended himself with ease, and the father fled in fear. Emer and CúChulainn finally were able to marry.

That's to say that CúChulainn's life became easy. A son he fathered while off training in Scotland came back into his life, bringing grief. CúChulainn takes on a variety of lovers and almost leaves Emer for one of them. In the end, though, CúChulainn returns to Emer. It's eventually Medb who brings about CúChulainn's death.

Again we see the theme. Love isn't smooth. It's rough and rocky. A man has to be strong enough to make it through the storms. A woman has to be strong enough to handle what life throws at the world.

Saint Brigid - Patroness of Ireland

OK, let's leave the blood-and-tears of the Ulster Cycle to move on into a real life character. Saint Brigid is worshipped across Ireland as the patron saint of Ireland. Many Irish homes feature a Saint Brigid's cross on a wall for good luck.

Saint Brigid was born around 452 in County Louth. She was purportedly born to Dubhthach, a chieftain, and one of his slave women, although not all researchers agree on this point. Brigid was attractive and intelligent, and as she matured she realized that she had no desire to marry. She refused all men who asked her. Her love was of knowledge and helping others, not of being a housewife and home-tender. She chose instead to be a nun at Druin Criadh. She created the Convent of Cill-Dara near a large oak tree. This area is now the town of Kildare.

Saint Brigid's convent became a center of learning and religion, that grew greatly both in size and reputation during her lifetime and after her death. In addition to her convent, she founded a monastery for men, and another for women. She became the Abbess of Kildare. She was in full charge of her holdings, and she also oversaw religious activities in other locations.

Saint Brigid was a contemporary of Saint Patrick, and the two were great friends. Together they converted thousands to Christianity, brought about great improvements in education, and increased the level of knowledge held by the people of Ireland.

Saint Brigid had a special focus on students and the arts. This focus was due to her great love for the arts and her enthusiastic encouragement of learning. She founded an art school which taught metalwork and illumination. Illumination refers to the beautiful colored writing styles used by monks of this age, such as in the Book of Kells.

When Saint Brigid died, she was buried in the Kildare Cathedral. On her feast day of February 1st many pilgrims would trek for hundreds of miles to come to worship there. When that area came under attack by Norse raiders, Saint Brigid's relics were moved to a place of safety. Now they are located in the Downpatrick Cathedral, along with items from Saint Columba and Saint Patrick.

Saint Brigid's passion for the arts and her desire to help others has inspired many poets, writers, and lovers over the ages. Lovers will pray to Saint Brigid for an honest and true partner. Poets will look to Saint Brigid for inspiration when they compose their sonnets.

Perhaps Saint Brigid can bring some Irish luck into your own life or romance!

A few of the symbols representing Saint Brigid include the Madonna lily, the oak tree, and the color white. Her feast day is February 1st.

St. Brigid's Bread (recipe is found later in the book)

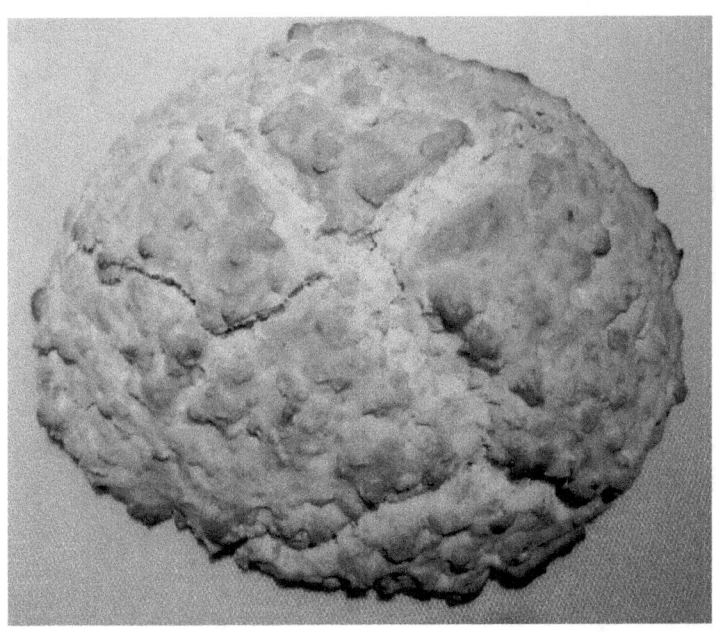

Saint Ultan wrote the following hymn for Saint Brigid, extolling her virtues and miracles:

In our island of Hibernia,

Christ was made

known to man

by the very great miracles

which he performed through

the happy virgin of celestial life,

famous for her merits

through the whole world.

Translation:

Christus in nostra insula

Que vocatur Hivernia

Ostensus est hominibus

Maximis mirabilibus

Que perfecit per felicem

Celestis vite virginem

Precellentem pro merito

Magno in numdi circulo.

The following is a prayer of Saint Brigid, supposedly penned by the woman herself. She was known for turning water into beer, or for having a single barrel of ale miraculously multiply into many to feed the clergy on festival days.

I wish I had a great lake of ale

for the King of kings,

and the family of heaven

to drink it through time eternal.

I wish I had the meats of belief

and genuine piety,

the flails of penance,

and the men of heaven in my house.

I would like casks of peace to be at their disposal,

vessels of charity for distribution,

caves of mercy for their company,

and cheerfulness to be in their drinking.

I would want Jesus also to be in their midst,

together with the three Marys of illustrious renown,

and the people of heaven from all parts.

I would like to be a tenant to the Lord,

so if I should suffer distress,

he would confer on me a blessing.

Amen.

Faeries

When Christianity swept through Ireland thanks to the efforts of people like Saint Brigid and Saint Patrick, the Irish still held on strongly to their spiritual roots. They venerated nature and the hidden creatures which shared their misty world. It's no surprise that in a landscape often swirling with fogs, the Irish treasured their rich belief in the faerie world.

Faeries figure strongly in Irish tales of love and romance. Faeries are often seducing away handsome men or attractive women to join their care-free worlds of dancing and singing.

Faeries were young, beautiful, usually female, and delightfully social. Faeries were fond of parties and gatherings.

Many Irish customs around dating and marriage exist to protect the young couple from jealous faeries.

The tie between faeries and weddings is quite strong. Many tales exist with this combination. Faeries love to celebrate and they adore all things beautiful. What better than a wedding to draw them in?

Legend has it that faeries who are attracted to a wedding will kidnap the bride and groom to have them celebrate in the faerie kingdom. The couple would be taken to *Tir Nan Og*, the faerie land which lies to the west of Ireland, in the mists. Here, springtime reigns eternal and no work ever need be done.

The bride and groom would lose all track of time and stay there for decades, not noticing the passage of time. When they finally escaped from the dream world. they would find their family long dead and their possessions gone.

Green is an unlucky color to wear at a wedding because the faeries were drawn to it. The faeries might lure away those green-wearing wedding guests to their hidden land.

While modern day Irish couples usually don't believe in the threat of a faerie kidnapping, they still take all of the proper precautions … just in case!

Leprechauns

Leprechauns were short, stubby male creatures, who came up to the height of your knee. They were solitary, loved complicated riddles, and often spent their time making shoes. The name Leprechaun came from the Gaelic words for one-shoe, since they were often spotted working on a shoe.

Leprechauns were mischievous and delighted in tormenting and disrupting the lives of humans.

You might think of the happy-go-lucky leprechaun from the cereal commercials. This is a far tamer version of the real thing! The actual leprechauns could be greedy, sharp-tongued, and delighted by causing all sorts of serious trouble.

Leprechauns were especially drawn to causing trouble for lovers. Nothing pleased them more than to cross up a couple in love. Couples who courted and planned a wedding took every step they could to ensure leprechauns would not cause mischief.

For example, Irish men would often wear breeches, which were a short form of pants which came to just past the knee. The fabric would be buttoned below the knee to hold it in place. The groom, on his wedding day, left his left knee button undone so the faeries would not realize the wedding was about to begin. That way they would not attend and disrupt it.

The groom also would carry his new bride over the threshold because the leprechauns lurked in that location, waiting to trip her and embarrass her.

The leprechaun's skill with riddles and puzzles was prized throughout Ireland. Tribes of faeries would use leprechauns to guard their faerie treasure. The faeries knew the leprechaun would be able to outwit anybody who came to steal it.

The luck of the leprechauns was legendary. Young lovers would often take complicated steps to bring some of this luck into their lives. Pink heather was thought to capture some leprechaun luck, as was a four leaf clover. Both were common tokens of affection for the Irish.

Banshees

You don't have to spend long in Ireland to see where the legends of banshees come from. Walk down a quiet country road on a misty night, with the fog swirling all around you, and the wind howling through the trees, and you'll be sure that the banshees are out!

Banshees are female and are strongly related to death. They either indicate someone's about to die or that someone who is dead is trying to get in touch with the living.

While in modern times we often equate death with black, in Irish tradition it was white or grey that a banshee would be seen in. Think of how a ghost is supposed to be white – this is the same mindset.

Relating to banshees, noble houses would sometimes hire "keeners" – female singers with piercing, soulful voices – to sing / cry at funerals. The powerful emotions brought out by that song was thought to relate to the cry of a banshee.

Irish Music and Song

"Gypsy rover, come over the hill,

down through the valley so shady

He whistled and he sang til the green woods rang

and he won the heart of a lady."

—The Whistling Gypsy, traditional

As far back as can be known, Ireland has been a country of music and song. CúChulainn, nephew to the famous king Conchobar mac Nessa, is famous for his heroic deeds. He once stated, "I care not whether I die tomorrow or next year, if only my deeds live after me."

For many Irish rulers, it was more important to be remembered through song and poem than to find success while they lived.

Harp

To accompany traditional stories, the first poets and story-tellers often played the harp. This stringed instrument could be made in a travel size, so that evenings spent around the campfire could be livened with entertainment. There were also large, majestic harps which had a permanent home in the keeps and castles of kings and nobles.

A harp was not a frivolous instrument. Harps were designed to accompany a storyteller who had epic tales to tell. It provided that "grander than life" atmosphere to the telling.

The harp would also provide elegant music during a stately dinner or an important ceremony. Harp music is excellent for quiet cocktail parties, engagement dinners, wedding ceremonies, and receptions.

Bodhran

Another traditional Irish instrument is the bodhran - a small hand drum made of wood and goat skin. Its use traces back to pre-Christianity as a rhythm instrument to accompany dancing and as a background for long poetic chanting.

This was and is a great dual- purpose instrument. It is useful for long sessions of storytelling and also for wild dancing and merrymaking.

Irish Pub Music

Eventually other musical newcomers, such as the flute and violin, joined the Irish music scene. The music-loving Irish would gladly stay up through the night to enjoy both dance and song. Irish pubs often close in the wee hours of the morning.

Irish weddings are known to last all night and into the morning as guests and celebrants enjoy the fine Irish music.

There are many excellent Irish CDs available today. The following pages contain just a few suggestions.

The Chieftains

I adore the Chieftains. I was privileged enough to meet them in Millstreet during a festival there. My family has a home in Millstreet and this was their "back yard." The Chieftains are warm, compassionate, and have been making fantastic music together since 1962. Simply superb musicians. Get any albums you can.

Clancey Brothers

This group began in the 1950s and quickly became quite popular. They helped share the traditional folk music of Ireland – drinking songs, sea shanties, and the like – with the world. Perfect for parties.

Van Morrison

Another great who's performed in Millstreet – he was simply spectacular live in that at-home setting. Beautiful vocals, soulful playing, he encompasses a different part of Ireland – the romantic, heartfelt man.

Enya / Clannad

These are clearly more "new age" and I adore them just the same. It is beautiful to hear the Gaelic language in all its flowing glory. There are some traditional ballads mixed in with their original works.

The Dubliners

A group along the lines of the Chieftains and the Clancey Brothers, the Dubliners also helped bring traditional, pub-style Irish music to the world.

There are of course thousands of other Irish bands in wide ranges of styles from pop to rock, from traditional to avant-garde. Give them all a listen, and support Irish music.

That being said, the core of Irish tradition is to participate. Irish wouldn't go to a pub to turn on the radio or bring in a DJ. They wanted to play the music themselves and dance to the live tunes. You don't have to be a world class artist. You just need to know how to hit a drum to participate.

If you're even in the tiniest bit musically inclined, pick up an instrument and begin to learn some of the folk tunes for yourself! You don't need to be an expert. It's OK to be a beginner. The way of the Irish is to delight in their friends and family bringing music into a quiet room.

Irish Marching Bands

If you've been to a St. Patrick's Day parade you're probably aware
that the Irish love for music definitely extends to marching bands. The
two most common forms are the bagpipes band and the brass band.

Bagpipes band use the bagpipe, as you might imagine. While many
people equate Scottish culture with bagpipes, the Irish have them as
well. The Irish bagpipes are known in modern times as Uilleann
pipes. They tend to have a "softer" sound than the Scottish war pipes.

For Irish brass bands, there is a history that ties them (and English
brass bands as well) to coal mines. A great movie on this topic, set in
England, is *Brassed Off*, starring Ewan McGregor.

Villages would have competitions and the bands would go from place
to place, delighting the spectators. In modern times we might equate
brass bands only with special parades, but in a time before TV and
radio a brass band was a great way to enjoy an afternoon with friends.

Here's Bob, in the center, with some of his band-mates at the St.
Patrick's Day parade in Worcester, MA. He's wearing the Aran
sweater his mom bought for him in Ireland during one of our trips
there.

Irish Recipes

"Half a loaf is better than no bread."

—Irish proverb

It's intriguing that the main dish most Americans associate with Irish Food isn't even an authentic Irish dish! That dish is Corned Beef and Cabbage. This dish was never served in Ireland. Here's the story.

When the Potato Famine happened from 1845 to 1851, millions of Irish immigrants flooded New York. These new Irish arrivals had little or no money. However, at Easter, there was a traditional dish that they wanted to have. This was boiled Irish bacon (ham rump) with a mix of vegetables. This hearty meal was a traditional feature of the served during Easter celebration.

The butchers of the area, seeing an opportunity, sold them the cheapest cut they had - corned beef. The Irish were resourceful and used this cut to try to bring back memories of home, adding in cabbage, which was also inexpensive. The resulting dish became popular with the Irish immigrants and spread into popular culture in America.

In fact, until recently, you could not find Corned Beef and Cabbage anywhere in Ireland. However, because so many American tourists would go to Ireland and demand it, some of the tourist spots do now indeed serve the dish! This recent development is an example of tourists thinking something was authentic, and causing the native culture to change to match their expectations.

Until recently, many Irish families could not afford to eat meat regularly. The native Irish were subsistence farmers, living on potatoes, carrots, bread, and butter. It was mostly the English lords of the land who could afford to eat better food. However, there were always meats for special occasions, and as the general population has become wealthier in recent years, meat has become a regular part of meals. The most popular meats are lamb, bacon, and fish. Salmon is especially desired, as it is thought to bring wisdom when eaten. There's even an Irish proverb about salmon:

A trout in the pot is better than a salmon in the sea.

Here are some recipes for you to try, to bring some Irish flavors into your life.

Saint Brigid's Bread

Saint Brigid is a Patron Saint of Ireland, and is well loved for her dedication to the arts and learning. Her feast day is February 1st, and this bread is often eaten then. This bread is also enjoyed during the rest of the year as a hearty part of a meal. For many Irish of times past, bread and butter might be the only thing eaten at a meal.

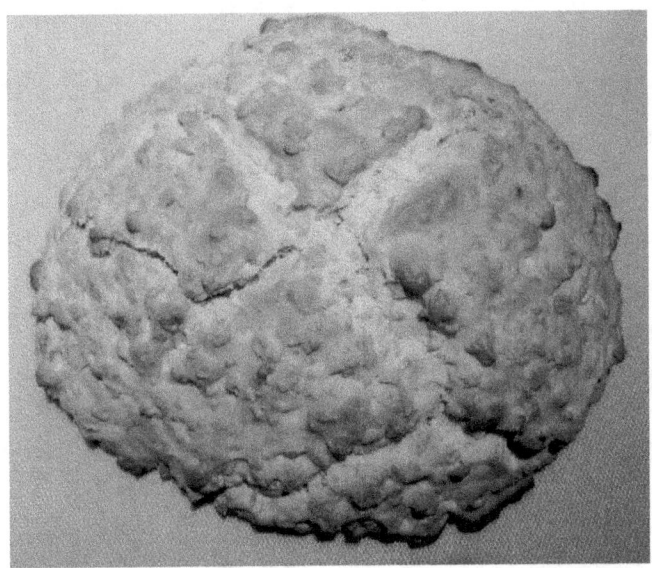

1 cup flour
1 Tbsp sugar
3/4 tsp baking powder
1/4 tsp salt
1/4 tsp baking soda
3 Tbsp butter
3/4 cup uncooked oats
1/2 cup buttermilk
1 egg

In a bowl, mix together the flour, sugar, baking powder, salt, and baking soda. Cut the butter into small pieces and blend it in to the dry ingredients. Stir in the oats. In a separate bowl, blend the buttermilk and egg together. Mix the two sets of ingredients together and form a dough ball.

Knead the dough until smooth (around 40 times) and shape into an 8-inch circle. Put this on a greased cookie sheet, and cut a cross shape into its top to honor Saint Brigid.

Bake at 425°F (218°C) for about 20 minutes.

Lamb Stew

One of the most loved Irish meats in the spring is lamb. Sheep are easy animals to raise in the rocky hills of the western coastline of Ireland. If you drive through the twisty roads of County Cork and Kerry in the spring, you'll find hundreds of sheep and lambs roaming the hills and roads. Don't be surprised by their colorful markings. Each sheep is spray-painted with a special color by its owner so that they can be sorted out even if flocks end up mingling during their days of wandering.

Here's a recipe for traditional lamb stew, which is just perfect for a cold, misty evening! Leftover stew can be reheated and enjoyed for several days after. The recipe also shows you just how resourceful the Irish were at reusing their ingredients.

6 pounds boneless lamb shoulder
1/2 cup flour
1 tsp salt
1/2 tsp black pepper
1/2 pound thickly sliced bacon
1 large yellow onion
cloves garlic
1/2 cup water
2 tsp sugar
4 cups beef stock
1 cup Chardonnay
bay leaf
1 tsp thyme
large onions
pounds potatoes
cups carrots

Cut the lamb into cubes about 2" on a side. Mix the lamb with the flour, salt, and pepper until it is well coated. Dice the bacon and sauté it in a pan. Remove the bacon bits but leave the fat behind. Brown the lamb in the fat. Remove the lamb from the pan, retaining the fat.

Peel and finely chop the yellow onion, and peel and finely chop the garlic cloves. Sauté these in the fat until they brown. Add in the water, and stir well.

Now put the lamb into a large pot, and pour in the garlic-onion-water from the pan. Add in the bacon bits as well. Next, mix in the sugar and beef stock. Cover the pot and simmer for 1 1/2 hours.

In a bowl, mix together the Chardonnay, bay leaf, and thyme. Peel and slice the remaining onions into cubes, and add these. Next peel and slice the potatoes into 1/2" cubes, and add the potato to the bowl. Finally, peel and slice the carrots into 1" cubes and add these. Mix together, and then pour entire mix into the pot. Cook for another 20 minutes.

Guinness Beef

One of my *favorite* dishes of all time in Ireland is Guinness Beef. The flavor is very rich and delicious, and it warms you right through on a chilly evening. The alcohol cooks out of the meal, so this is fine for all ages.

1/4 pound butter
1 pound beef chuck
1 large sweet onion
1/4 tsp salt
1/4 tsp pepper
1/4 tsp parsley
1/4 tsp sage
1/4 tsp thyme
1 bay leaf
1 pint Guinness stout
1 cup beef stock
4 medium potatoes
4 large carrots

Warm the butter in a skillet. Cube the beef chuck into 1 1/2" cubes and brown them. Remove the beef. Cut the onion into cubes, and brown it in the butter. After 3 minutes, add the beef back in, plus the salt, pepper, parsley, sage, thyme and the bay leaf. Now pour in the pint of Guinness and the beef stock. Bring to a boil.

Transfer the food to a baking dish and bake, uncovered, at 350°F (177°C) for an hour. Peel the potatoes and cut them into 2" cubes, and do the same to the carrots. Add them into the pan and cook for another 45 minutes. Make the juice into a gravy with flour and milk.

Irish Soda Bread

A favorite of many, Irish soda bread goes perfectly with Guinness Beef! It's also the perfect breakfast bread with a cup of tea. We love making this – it's hard to make it last the week.

Yeast:
2 tsp dry yeast
1 Tbsp sugar
1/4 cup warm water

Bread:
3 cups bread flour
1 cup graham flour
1 Tbsp baking powder
4 tsp salt
1/2 cup sugar
1/2 cup (1 stick) butter
1 cup raisins
2 eggs
1 1/2 tsp baking soda
1 1/2 cup buttermilk

3 Tbsp Caraway seeds (optional)

First, ready the yeast. Make sure the water is lukewarm so it activates but does not kill the yeast. Mix the water in with the yeast and the sugar and let it sit for a half hour in a bowl. This is going to rise a fair amount – make sure it's in a substantial container.

Meanwhile, mix together both types of flour, plus the baking powder, salt, and sugar. Cut the butter into small pieces. What we do is cut the stick into patties, but leaving them all stuck together, and then cut the entire stick down its length. You don't want to melt the butter – you need it to retain its firmness. Blend it into the mixture. The butter won't vanish completely at this point, but that's OK. The lumps will be worked out during the kneading stage.

Now mix in the raisins.

In yet another bowl, mix together two eggs, baking soda, and buttermilk. Now blend the flour mixture into this, and then blend the yeast mixture in. Mix all together into dough.

Knead for about five minutes on a flowered surface, until it is no longer sticky. Add flour as you go if necessary to get it into that nice bread dough / softly tacky state.

Form into a ball. Put this dough ball into a greased bowl, cover with a towel or wax paper, and let it rise somewhere room temperature for an hour.

Shape the ball of dough into an 8-inch circle, and put it onto a greased cookie sheet. Much like with the Saint Brigid's Bread, cut a cross shape into the top of it. Brush the top with melted butter, and sprinkle the Caraway seeds on top if you like those.

Bake at 375°F (190°C) for 45 minutes.

We do this in a toaster oven sometimes so we break it into two halves and do each half for 35 minutes. You can also, of course, halve the recipe. The picture you see here, with the bread taking up an entire dinner plate, is of the half loaf. So they get quite large!

Corned Beef and Cabbage

We make Corned Beef and Cabbage in our crockpot every St. Patrick's Day – and for a few weeks on either side of the holiday, too. I love the taste of the "grey" corned beef, while Bob finds that too mild and prefers the "red" version. Since he's the cook in the house, you can imagine which one we tend to get :). Still, I continue to lobby for the grey!

An added treat with this (and any crockpot recipe, really) is that the entire house smells delicious while this is cooking.

We have a 6 ½ quart crockpot explicitly so we can make these large corned beef meals with it. If your crockpot is smaller than that, you might want to reduce these amounts proportionally so your corned beef can fit within what you have available.

Ingredients:
5 pounds corned beef
1 medium head cabbage
1-2 pounds carrots
1 larger-than-softball rutabaga
1 large yellow onion
Few inches celery
Pickling spice

Optional:
1 pint stout beer
¼ cup Splenda brown sugar

Cut the corned beef, if necessary, to get it to fit into the crock pot. Put it in fat-side up. Add in the spice. The corned beef we get comes with those spices, or you can use your own if you'd rather do that.

Peel the rutabaga. Cut the carrots and rutabaga into fork-sized pieces and sprinkle them around. Cube the onion and celery and add those in.

You don't need to add any water to this – it will add its own. Start cooking on low for four hours.

At this point (the half-way point) you can add the cabbage in, if it'll fit. If it won't, take out some of the liquid and add that to water in a stovetop pot to start the cabbage cooking. For the cabbage, we half it, then quarter it, then eighth it. Don't put it in whole :). It'll turn into a super-heated bowling ball.

This is where you would add the stout and brown sugar into the crockpot if you wished to use those.

Cook on low for another four hours.

Enjoy! For us this makes two servings :). OK, that includes leftovers.

An Irish Breakfast

Soda Bread is a great way to start the day. Many Irish eat this each morning with fresh butter spread on it, with a cup of hot tea. Tea and bread for breakfast is an Irish classic.

Another traditional Irish breakfast would start with fresh bacon circles fried in a pan. Next, in the same fat you would cook fried eggs. Finally, in the same pan you'd quick-fry small circular slices of tomato – Roma tomatoes work well — so they became crisp. This meal is very, very tasty and uses only a single breakfast pan.

It's interesting that while other cultures look on breakfast as a romantic event, the Irish see this as a pragmatic, important start to the day of work. In fact, there's an Irish proverb that says:

"Marriages are all happy –

it's having breakfast together that causes all the trouble!"

Even so, have some fun at your breakfasts, and do them Irish-style!

Irish Flowers

"My wild Irish Rose,

The sweetest flow'r that grows,

You may search ev'rywhere,

But none can compare

With my wild Irish Rose."

—Chauncey Olcott, 1899

Ireland is a country of green fields, green meadows, and green forests. Any bouquet of flowers presented to reflect Ireland would do well to have an abundance of green fern, ivy, clover, and leaf in it.

Ivy is especially loved by the Irish and is commonly found both in lovers' bouquets and bridal floral arrangements. To the Irish, ivy stands for a faithful and true lover.

The shamrock – or Irish clover - is well known as the symbol of Ireland and was used by Saint Patrick to explain the nature of the trinity to Irish natives. He showed how the three leaves of the shamrock were separate but formed one plant. Shamrocks can be used both for general Irish significance and for holding a special place in any church-related floral arrangements.

A four leaf clover is a special mutation of clover. They used to be a rare 'mistake' in a patch of regular three-leaf clover. The mutation rate is one in 10,000! Nowadays there are four leaf clovers bred specially for the market. Because the four leaf clover was so unusual, the Irish took it as a lucky sign of the leprechaun. Someone finding a four leaf clover was sure to have a lucky event happen soon. Try giving your dear one a four leaf clover in a card, to bring them some luck along with your love!

In addition to the verdure of ivy, clover, and fern, the Irish also love colorful flowers. Flowers of any shape, size, and color are enjoyed with equal pleasure. The Irish do have a special place in their hearts for wildflowers - especially those which grow wild around cottages and in fields. The Irish enjoy the beauty of nature over the cultivated care of a hot-house.

OK, this photo gets a story :). On one trip to Ireland we attended the wedding of a relative. This cute little bunny rabbit was on the lawn of the reception building, eating dandelions. It would bite off the bottom of the stem and then suck the dandelion into its mouth like a strand of spaghetti. I've never seen any other rabbit do that!

Roses

Roses are a symbol of love in just about every culture, and this is especially true in Ireland. Climbing roses are found around many Irish cottages, and roses are often brought to a girl by the lad that loves her. References to roses can be found in many traditional Irish songs.

"My Wild Irish Rose" is probably the most famous song and is a traditional wooing tune.

Foxglove

Another popular flower for the Irish is the foxglove. The name of the foxglove comes from the Welsh language. The "foxes-glew" was a musical instrument made from bells hung on an arch. For the Irish, the Foxglove flower stands for youth, innocence, and dreams. It was also an important medical plant for the Irish.

Foxglove was often given by a young suitor to his love to show that he treasured her sweet youth and that he hoped to fulfill all of her dreams of the future.

Bells of Ireland

The Bells of Ireland (*Moluccelia laevis*) are lovely, green flowers which are thought to bring the luck of the Irish.

These bells are traditionally given when people start a new project. This could be for a new job, a new home, going steady, or becoming engaged.

Heather

Heather comes in several colors and each has a different meaning. Pink heather is for bringing the luck of the leprechauns into your life. Purple heather is for admiration or passion - perfect for a loved one. White heather is a flower of protection, safety, and security. This is perfect for a housewarming gift.

Not all flowers bring luck and love. Two flowers that are avoided by the Irish are the lilac and apple blossoms. Both of these flowers bring bad luck and unhappiness. Be sure to keep these far from the ones you love!

Some flowers send complex messages. For examples, rhododendrons are enjoyed for their beauty. For the Irish, they also symbolized a need for caution or careful attention. While this wouldn't be ideal for a bridal bouquet, it could be appropriate for a relationship that is at a turning point, to indicate you both need to pay more attention to caring for each other.

Herbs

While flowers are appreciated for their beauty, the Irish are also a very practical people. They would always prefer to have something that was useful *and* lovely. To have a flower that was difficult to care for and died quickly made little sense to them.

For this reason, herbs and herb gardens were extremely important to the Irish. One of the key herbs for romance is myrtle. This is an herb which brings luck and love to Irish brides. An Irish bride would carry myrtle until the wedding ceremony was finished. She would then give some of the myrtle to each of her bridesmaids.

Medieval brides would wear a wreath of herbs to help protect them from the unwanted attention of faeries. The herbs would, at the same time, attract luck and fertility.

Bring some luck and love into your own life by keeping an Irish plant or herb garden nearby!

Finding a Mate

Flirting and dating in Ireland was a national pastime, from the enjoyment of great food to the evenings of music. In pre-Christian Ireland, dating and taking lovers was part of growing up. Couples would only marry when they wished to have children and pass along possessions to a new generation. The decision of who to marry was completely up to the pair, since each would retain ownership of the land they brought into the marriage, and would retain their independence in most other ways as well.

When Christianity came into the Isles, it brought a new emphasis on the commitment to a relationship which lasted a lifetime. It also brought with it the idea that anything belonging to the wife now became the property of the husband. This caused a large shift in how marriage affected family fortunes and land ownership. The emphasis and importance placed on marriage grew immensely.

Read on to learn more about the folklore involved in choosing a spouse, and how things have changed over the years.

Folklore about Future Spouses

Every culture has their sayings and folklore about determining whom you will marry. Marriage is one of the most important stages in the 'expected life path' of a young person, and much attention is focused on it. Ireland is no exception!

Usually it was the women using love charms and tests, not the men. This was because during much of Ireland's history a woman over twenty was seen as a hindrance, an old maid who had not yet 'caught a man.' She often considered herself a burden to her family, and she used every means she could to divine how to find herself a man of her own. Also, since women rarely initiated the engagement process, she was at the mercy of the man's intentions.

For a man, it was common to remain unmarried for many years, as he had his work, his extended family, and perhaps a battle or two to win. It was common for an older man to marry a younger woman, so he could choose a young wife whenever he decided to settle down.

A man could marry when he wished, but for a woman, the clock began ticking early in life.

Here are some love charms and traditions well known in Ireland.

Chestnuts

One of the oldest types of love charm involved chestnuts. The curious maiden would choose one chestnut for herself and one for her love. The pair of chestnuts was placed side by side at the front of an open fire.

If the two chestnuts remained side by side in the fire, it meant that the love was true and would stand the test of time.

If the lover's chestnut leapt away, it meant he would make the maiden unhappy.

If the maiden's own chestnut jumped away, it meant that the maiden would end up not loving him.

The Wood Stack

One love-sensing technique involved the stack of wood used to keep the house warm. At midnight on Halloween or on the summer solstice, the girl would sneak out to the log pile. She would draw out a stick in the dark. The shape of the stick represented her future husband.

If the stick was twisty and bent, it meant she'd marry an old, bent man.

If it was straight and true, her husband would also be young and strong.

The Salty Egg

Some Irish methods of seeking knowledge on romance seem to make little sense. For example, one tradition instructed the maiden to boil an egg, and when it was hard-boiled, cool it. The maiden would then cut off the top of the egg and scoop out the yolk. With the egg now hollow, she would fill the egg with salt.

In the evening, the girl would eat the entire salt-filled egg in one gulp. This would of course make the girl quite thirsty! She would then go to bed without drinking anything, and without speaking to anyone.

If her true love appeared to her in a dream offering her water to drink, it meant she could not trust him!

The Wedding Cake

At least this tradition gives more positive information about one's future spouse. With this tradition, when an unmarried person attends a wedding, they're supposed to break off a small piece of the wedding cake. They then ask the bride to let them pass that small piece through her new wedding ring (she has to take it off for a moment, of course).

Now the single person heads home with their 'charmed' bit of wedding cake. They put it under their pillow at night.

This should cause the person to dream about the person who will end up marrying them!

Growing into Love

The Irish have many proverbs that encourage couples that the best is yet to come. The idea that couples 'grow into love' is very common.

Two proverbs are:

The old pipe gives the sweetest smoke.

The older the fiddle the sweeter the tune.

St. Patrick's Cathedral, Dublin

Charming a Lover

This poem, "The Maiden's Plight," was written in the 1700s by Brian Merriman in County Clare. It pokes fun at the various charms young girls would use to seek a husband..

It demonstrates that the quest for love is not a new one!

'I fasted three canonical hours
To try and come round the heavenly powers;
I washed my shift where the stream was deep
To hear a lover's voice in sleep;
Often I swept the woodstack bare,
Burned bits of my frock, my nails, my hair,
Up the chimney stuck the flail,
Slept with a spade, without avail;
Hid my wool in the limekiln late
And my distaff behind the churchyard gate;
I had flax on the road to halt coach or carriage
And haycocks stuffed with heads of cabbage.
And night and day on the proper occasions
invoked Old Nick and all his legions;
But t'was all no good and I'm broken hearted
For here I'm back at the place I started;
And this is the cause of all my tears
I am fast in the rope of the rushing years,
With age and need in lessening span,
And death beyond, and no hope of a man.'

Choosing a Proper Spouse – an Ancient View

Giorraíonn beirt bóthar

Two people shorten the road.

—Gaelic Proverb (meaning the trip passes more pleasantly)

According to ancient Irish traditions, marriage was all about creating children. For the pre-Christian Irish, marriage could be broken if the two were unhappy, without any loss of honor or pride. Many folk stories dating from these times tell of couples divorcing and then ending up quite contentedly with their second or third mates.

Women at this time had full say in who they loved and married, and kept control of any land, money or other possessions they owned. It was understood that a pair who married (instead of living as lovers) was doing so in order to have children to inherit their property. A woman was expected to deny a man if he was:

* Physically unable to father children

* Had no land

* Was a religious man sworn to celibacy

* A "claenain" - a man who shows he cannot be trusted

Stories told about these days often emphasize how love matches were important. In many a tale, the woman would expressly go against her father's wishes and marry the man she loved. As women were independent, and had their own money, land and property, they could choose who to join with and who to leave without any 'loss of land' issues for the family. A proverb from the time says, "There'll be white blackbirds before an unwilling woman ties the knot."

As Christianity came into Ireland, it began to introduce the notion that marriage was forever. This was a difficult change for many Irish, who were used to joining and leaving unions as they grew and changed. They developed the 'handfasting' tradition to help them make sure a partnership really worked before marrying.

In handfasting, the pair would have a ceremony, wrapping a ribbon around their hands, to show they would seriously attempt a marriage for a year. They would test out their marriage compatibility, to see if they really were meant for each other. If things did not work out they would simply move on and look for a more suitable partner, with no harm done to either one. If things did work, they would take the next step and make the vow for life.

When Christianity swept the nation, other aspects of marriage and relationships changed. Saint Patrick brought in a powerful form of Christianity to the Irish. With it came the sense that virginity was sacred, and that marriage was a permanent, religious vow that could never be broken. Also, Christianity introduced the notion that men were the responsible heads of the family, and women should look to them for leadership. Women no longer owned property or money – when she married, all she owned became the property of her husband, under his control. This was a big change from previous beliefs.

Now marriage became a one-time-only vow, and it could seriously affect how property was distributed amongst families. Women became liabilities instead of equal partners - a daughter would not inherit the land, and in fact now would have to be provided with a dowry in order for a man to take her. When she was "given away" to another man, in essence the family would lose her usefulness around the house, and also lose a fair amount of money and property in the form of her dowry. If the family planned things properly, they might get in return an increase in status and rank, depending on their daughter's spouse.

The finances and land involved, and the man's new power in the family unit, led to the fathers looking on marriages as 'financial arrangements', and planning the marriages of their children. A tender father might consider the feelings of his son or daughter, but the more realistic ones would pay attention to how this union would affect the entire family's financial situation and standing in the village. The two people marrying would then pray for a happy life together, and be content in the knowledge that they were helping their family as best they could.

Mate-Choosing

Life in Ireland was rarely easy, so observations like "she has a pretty face" were not high on the list of reasons to marry someone. A pretty face could easily turn into a shrewish wife that was lazy around the house, a wasteful spender at the markets, and a horrible parent. The Irish were very practical — one of their proverbs says

"If you have one pair of good soles

it's better than two pairs of good uppers."

Instead of relying on looks, which fade over time, Irish men and women would instead watch for valuable traits in each other. When the two individuals had the choice, they would choose a mate based on real life skills — how well could she cook and clean? How well could he farm and handle animals? They had to work well together, and talk together, to manage their household and family well.

In the early days of Irish history, both husband and wife had equal say in the household, and laws made it very clear that both had a shared voice and a shared hand in their wealth. If the pair divorced, each would take his or her own belongings and go on with life.

As Christianity grew in favor, things began to change. The role of women lessened, and the use of marriage as a land-match rather than a child-bearing-choice came into being. Soon, the choice of who to marry was not left to the boy and girl, but was in the hands of the fathers.

The fathers would get together at the harvest fairs or markets that were held, and while they negotiated the sale of their crops and animals, they would also negotiate the marriage of their children. Often, official matchmakers would help out by being an impartial go-between, setting the dowries and helping resolve arguments.

The oldest girl would have to marry first, and then each younger girl would follow. The fathers would determine how much of a dowry would have to be offered before the groom's father would accept her, and the groom's father would have to prove he had enough land, cattle, and other wealth to ensure her children would be well cared for. Often, if the market drew people from various villages, the boy and girl would not even know each other before the contract was complete.

Customs evolved to help keep the process orderly. For example, in County Limerick, the eligible young men would wear a shamrock on their clothes to show they were 'in the running'. Sometimes the homes of available girls would be marked with blue, since blue at the time was the sign of purity.

While the bride's father usually paid to have her 'taken off of his hands', there were a few instances of the groom paying a bride-price, or "coibche". This would occur if he was very poor, perhaps a youngest son in a large family without land, and was trying to 'work up' in the world by marrying a well-off bride. He would promise to work whatever land his father-in-law granted to him and turn it into a successful farm. He would then pay set amounts to the father of his bride in installments over the years. This would reimburse the father in law for the acquisition of the land.

These marriage arrangements were hammered out in open fairs, and completed in nearby pubs. The sealing of the vows between the boy and girl often took place on the couple's new homestead, or in an outdoor place of value to the village. The local village leader still held the position of final approval in an area, even as the church moved in, and marrying the couple was his honor and responsibility.

The customs varied from town to town. In Comillane is a pillar stone, and couples would join hands through a hole in the stone while the local chieftain married them. A similar pillar exists near Dingle. It was only much later as Christianity took a stronger hold on Ireland that the church became a part of the process.

Irish children at this time were raised to dream of love, but to believe in the value of hard work and supporting the family. They would go into this marriage with high hopes for tenderness and love, but with a pragmatic attitude that it *could* work if only they put the time and energy into it. And they were happy knowing that this marriage would bring wealth or rank to their families, and that they were doing their part in ensuring their family's success.

Courting and Dating the Irish Way

Molly dear now did you hear the news that's going 'round

Down in a corner of my heart a love is what you've found

Every time I look into your Irish eyes so blue

They seem to whisper, "Darling boy, my love is all for you."

—Irish Molly O, Traditional

Romantic courtship and the Irish culture go hand in hand. Everything about Ireland seems to speak of the true love a man has for his mate. There are the gently misty mornings with fresh tea and warm bread. There are the long, peaceful, horse-and-carriage tours of Killarney, with beautiful landscapes and bird song. There's the ringing toast with gorgeous hand-made crystal of Wexford by the quiet fire of a peat log. There's the world-recognized symbol of loyalty, the Claddagh rings of Galway Bay.

All of these Irish visions bring to mind images of tenderness, caring, and joy. It is easy for young lovers, newlywed couples, and long-together spouses to become enraptured with the charm. Any couple traveling across the Irish landscape will easily feel swept away by its romance.

Bring this atmosphere of Irish Romance to your own relationship! Read through the following pages to learn more about the flowers, songs, recipes, and traditions of courting and dating in Ireland.

A History of Dating in Ireland

"O, rattlin' roarin' Willie, o, he held to the fair

An' for to sell his fiddle an' buy some other ware

But parting wi' his fiddle, the saut tear blin't his e'e

And rattlin' roarin' Willie, ye're welcome hame to me."

—Rattlin' Roarin' Willie, Traditional

Most of Ireland is comprised of rural and fishing communities which have existed for hundreds of years. Young men and women grew up knowing everyone in town. They would see one another in church, in the market, and at the many dances and festivals. Groups of friends would go out together to make or listen to music. They would gather in the evenings to share in storytelling and singing songs. There was always a great appreciation for simple fun – in the sharing in the songs and poetry of their culture. Dating often became the natural progression as fun-seeking friends spent more and more time together.

Dating was about finding a best friend. The Irish would seek out mates with whom they had fun, whose company they enjoyed. At the same time, the Irish knew that life was challenging. Just look at the way their folklore stories tended to run! Therefore, they wanted a partner who was up to the bad times as well as the good. When they'd been children, they were heavily involved in the chores and tasks of the home and farm. Now that they were older, they knew well what life would require of them as responsible adults.

The man would want a wife who could help raise the animals, tend the garden, and keep any children fed and cared for. The woman would want a husband who would bring in a good catch, till the fields, and mend the fences. Both the man and woman would want a partner who could laugh with them in the morning, dance with them in the evening, and share in stories with their children as the peat fires dwindled to embers. The Irish knew the meaning of hard work - and they also thoroughly enjoyed the fun moments they had together.

One dating custom of Christian Ireland which intrigues many modern couples is that of "bundling." This dating routine was practiced by many other cultures of the time as well. In any culture that encouraged couples to stay virgins until they married, there has been the resulting struggle of the young couples who wanted to enjoy the pleasure of contact before the wedding ceremony. The Irish found a perfect compromise in "bundling" the two.

The dating couple, when they become serious, was allowed to sleep in the same bed at one of the family's homes. However, each of the pair was "bundled" - wrapped either in bedclothes or blankets, so that they could be close, but not actually caress one another. This gave the couple the contentment of snuggling together for the night and whispering to each other all night long. It also gave the parents the knowledge that the young adults were somewhere safe, under a watchful eye, and engaging in pleasant but proper embraces.

Bring some of the fun of Irish dating into your own world! In the following pages you'll learn about the colors, flowers, foods and sayings of Ireland.

Liven up your own life and love!

Irish Harvest Knots

For most of Ireland's history, until very recently, harvesting food was a critical part of the yearly cycle. If the harvest went poorly, people could die. So men and women shared the effort to make sure it went smoothly.

As women gathered up the grain or straw they would often take stray stalks and weave them into flowers or spiral designs. They'd tuck them into their hair or hook them on their dress as a decoration.

Men and women would then give these as tokens of affection to those they cared for.

A flower is one shape to try, as that always has romantic connotations in every culture. Another shape is a double ring. Simply create a long braid and then loop it around twice.

Note that separate from this, there was usually a celebration when the very last sheaf was harvested. This meant the end of the work and the beginning of the fun! So that last sheaf was carefully paid attention to and a special person would be chosen to ceremonially take it down.

Romantic Locations

Often there was a special location that young maidens would retreat to in order to fast and pray for a good husband. This location would vary from village to village. Often it was a sacred grove or special spring.

For example, girls near Tramore Bay would go down to "The Metal Man," an iron warning marker indicating dangerous rocks. They would go around it three times to pray for a marriage.

A common pilgrimage was to Lough Derg, where Saint Patrick had his forty days of fasting.

Standing stones are often seen as symbols of fertility and love, from their phallic shape.

Doagh Hole Stone

The Doagh Hole Stone deserves special mention. This is a standing stone located over the Six Mil Water valley. I love standing stones and have felt the power of visiting Stonehenge and other sacred sites. There are just something about standing stones. But the Doagh Hole Stones is one of the very few stones that have a hole through it.

For centuries the tradition has been that the couple stands on either side of the stone. One partner (traditionally the woman) reaches her hand through the hold. The other partner than takes it. They pledge to love each other eternally.

The Colors of Ireland

"Red is the rose that in yonder garden grows

Fair is the lily of the valley

Clear is the water that flows from the Boyne

But my love is fairer than any."

—Red is the Rose, traditional

You might think that the Irish national color is green and that it has always been green. Certainly, Ireland is known for its forty shades of green, and anybody who has visited Ireland might say that there are well over one hundred. From the misty leaves of Cork to the verdant fields of Kerry, from the grasslands of Wexford to the seas of the Aran Islands, there are myriad shades of green that no painting has yet captured.

Still, it was only in the 1800s that green became the national color of Ireland. For the hundreds of years before that, Ireland was known for its blue and gold. Blue was the color of St. Patrick, a much-loved saint of Ireland. Gold was the color of the harp, the symbol of Irish culture.

If you are planning to decorate or throw a party, but neither green nor blue and gold suit you, another choice would be to use the current flag colors - orange, white, and green. These are the colors of the flag of the Irish Republic, adopted in the early 1900s.

You could even use the colors the Irish people enjoy in their own decorating. Pastel colors are extremely popular in Ireland. Many homes in Ireland are now painted in pastel colors, especially in the Cork and Kerry regions. You can walk down many seaside lanes and main streets and see the rows of homes, each a different, soft color, reflecting the gentle mists that sweep along the walkways.

Choosing colors to wear and decorate with was often of personal importance to a particular Irish family. It is true that, in modern days, recognizing their nationality as Irish is of great significance to the Irish people. It was not that long ago, though, that clans would fight fiercely with clans, and counties with counties. To many, still, the clan and family colors are what are worn with pride.

Here are some of the more common surnames in Ireland and the colors they would wear.

If your name is not listed here, you may want to research your family's colors. You could introduce those colors into your environment and share in the pride of your ancestors.

Note that an O or O' in front of a name simply meant "grandson of."

Brennan: red and gold
Brown: yellow and black
Boyle: yellow and green
Burke: yellow and red
Byrne: red and white
Callaghan: green and white
Campbell: gold, black, and blue
Carroll: black and gold
Clarke: green and yellow
Collins: red and gold
Connell: green, white, and brown
Connolly: black and silver
Connor: green, white, and brown
Daly: black, white, yellow, and red
Doherty: red, white, and green
Doyle: blue, orange, red, and white
Duffy: green and gold
Dunne: blue and gold
Farrell: green and gold
Fitzgerald: red and white
Flynn: blue, white, and orange
Gallagher: black, white, and green

Johnston: white, black, and gold
Hayes: white and green
Healy: blue and white
Hughes: blue and white
Kelly: blue and white
Kennedy: silver, red, and black
Lynch: blue and gold
MacCarthy: red and white
Maguire: green, white, and red
Mahony: red, white, blue, and gold
O'Malley: red and yellow
Martin: blue and white
Meaney: silver and green
Moore: green and yellow
Murphy: red, white, black, and gold
Murray: blue and yellow
Nolan: red and white
O'Brien: red, white and gold
O'Donnell: yellow and red
O'Neill: red, white and blue
Quinn: red and white
Reilly: green and yellow
Ryan: red and white
See: silver and blue
Shea: blue and gold
Smith: white and green
Sullivan: red, yellow, and green
Sweeney: black, yellow, and green
Thompson: yellow and blue
Tucker: blue, yellow, and silver
Walsh: white, red, and black
White: white and red

Irish Love Poetry

The most beautiful music of all is the music of what happens.
—Irish proverb

Poets have always held a special place in Irish history. Poets wield great power and often sat at the right hand of the King. It was through their words, after all, that the King would live forever through history.

Great honor was given to poets and to their epics. The Book of Kells shows the talents of those who maintained the written word.

The power of the poets is relayed through the many folk tales of the Irish. Often, if the woman was swayed away from her husband, it was the romantic words of a poet which caught her heart.

Poems were not kept apart from normal folk. Poems were a normal, natural part of life. Tales were often told in poem form, because the rhythm and rhyme made for a gentle sound when the story was relayed before a flickering fire.

Poems were songs and songs poems. The two intertwined and were loved by all.

Poetic tales were told at pubs and around the peat fires of home. Irish farm boys would compose poems to their girlfriends, and she would respond in verse. All Irish – young and old - knew the great poetic tales of the kings and queens who had come before.

Isibeul ní Mhic Cailín

Here is a poem written by Isibeul ní Mhic Cailín in old Gaelic, in the Middle Ages. The poem is titled "Mairg darab galar an grádh," or "Love is a Sad Sickness."

It was translated by Maureen O'Brien, and Maureen has graciously allowed me to share this with you.

First, here is Maureen's literal translation of the lines.

Mairg darab galar an grádh,	Love is a sad sickness —
gibé fath fá n-abraim é	When speaking to him,
	whatever the cause,
is deacair sgarthain re a pháirt;	It is a hardship to separate
	after time together.
truagh an cás a bhfuilim féin.	Pity my own blood's case.
An grádh-soin tugas gan fhios,	This love of mine came
	without [my] knowledge;
ós é mo leas gan a luadh,	my benefits came over him
	without mention.
muna fhaghad furtacht tráth,	For us delay departure
	an hour,
biaidh mo bhláth go tana truagh.	If my flower would, till a
	time of pity.
An fear-soin dá dtugas grádh,	This man of mine —
	love came, for him,

'S nách féadaim a rádh ós aird,

and I cannot say from what

direction;

dá gcuire sé mise i bpéin,

though buried, it's myself

in pain,

go madh dó féin bhus

Till I burn myself with

céad mairg!

   a hundred sorrows!

Here is Maureen's poetic translation of the meaning behind the poem:

A sorrowful disease is love.

No matter why or what we've spoken of,

After togetherness, it's hard to part.

Pity the case of my own heart.

Without my knowing, this love came to me;

And I did good to him unspokenly.

For us, this parting for one hour delay;

Till pity's time, I would my flower stay.

It was for him, this man of mine, love came

And out of which direction, I can't name.

And though I bury it, I am in pain

Till I burn with a hundred sorrows' flame!

Thomas Moore

Thomas Moore was born on May 28, 1779, in Dublin, Ireland. By 1793 his works were already being printed. He went on to Trinity College and was part of the rebellion of the United Irishmen in 1798. He saw several of his friends die or be sent off in exile. He wrote a great deal of poetry as well as other works.

Thomas traveled abroad, spending time in Europe, Bermuda, Canada, and the United States. He wrote poems about each of these locations – often speaking out against slavery. He married Bessy Dyke and was quite content with her. Sadly, though, all five of their children died before he passed away in 1852.

Many of the works he wrote deal with love and romance. Here is *The Young May Moon*

The young May moon is beaming, love,

The glow-worm's lamp is gleaming, love;

   How sweet to rove

   Through Morna's grove,

When the drowsy world is dreaming, love!

Then awake!—the heavens look bright, my dear,

'Tis never too late for delight, my dear;

   And the best of all ways

   To lengthen our days

Is to steal a few hours from the night, my dear!

Now all the world is sleeping, love,

But the Sage, his star-watch keeping, love,

And I, whose star

More glorious far

Is the eye from that casement peeping, love.

Then awake!—till rise of sun, my dear,

The Sage's glass we'll shun, my dear,

Or in watching the flight

Of bodies of light

He might happen to take thee for one, my dear!

William B. Yeats

William B Yeats was born in 1865, just over a decade after Moore passed away. He was born to an artistic family and was encouraged from his early years to express himself in painting and words.

Yeats built a reputation for his poetry and his love of mysticism. In 1889, in his early twenties, he became infatuated with Maud Gonne, a self-assured fan of his. He proposed to her several times, but she refused, and she married a man Yeats hated. She then converted to Catholicism. Yeats was crushed that his muse would abandon him so.

Gonne's marriage didn't work out, Yeats finally had his one night of pleasure with her – and their relationship fell apart. This long, tragic situation had a great impact on Yeats.

The Abbey Theater was founded in 1899 and Yeats was closely involved with them for the rest of his life.

In 1916, 51-year-old Yeats married 25-year-old Georgie Hyde-Lees out of a desire to create heirs. They did have two children, although Yeats continued to have affairs with other women, but it seems his marriage was a happy one.

In 1919 Yeats wrote "Her Praise" about Maud Gonne; it is shown on the next page.

Yeats won The Nobel Prize for Literature in 1923, and continued to write well-received poetry for many years after.

Yeats passed away in 1939.

Her Praise

She is foremost of those that I would hear praised.

I have gone about the house, gone up and down

As a man does who has published a new book,

Or a young girl dressed out in her new gown,

And though I have turned the talk by hook or crook

Until her praise should be the uppermost theme,

A woman spoke of some new tale she had read,

A man confusedly in a half dream

As though some other name ran in his head.

She is foremost of those that I would hear praised.

I will talk no more of books or the long war

But walk by the dry thorn until I have found

Some beggar sheltering from the wind, and there

Manage the talk until her name come round.

If there be rags enough he will know her name

And be well pleased remembering it, for in the old days,

Though she had young men's praise and old men's blame,

Among the poor both old and young gave her praise.

— Yeats, 1919. The Wild Swans at Coole

Irish Gaelic Words and Phrases

tha am posadh coltach ri seillean —

tha mil ann 's tha gath ann

marriage is like a bee —

it contains both honey and a sting

The language Irish Gaelic, also known as Irish or Gaeilge, is a richly musical language. YouTube provides a wealth of examples of Irish Gaelic to enjoy. Musicians like Clannad and Enya have songs written in Irish Gaelic.

If you wish to learn Irish Gaelic, there are a variety of books and audio instruction on the subject. There are also many web pages which can help guide you through the language. I'd highly suggest going with an instruction set that involves audio, so you can hear the sounds. It's incredibly difficult to make guesses at proper sounds based on reading written descriptions of them.

The schools in Ireland are making a renewed effort to teach the young people the language, so it does not become lost.

Here are some words that might come in handy while you work on further studies. As a quick pronunciation help, here is a guide to the vowels in Irish Gaelic. Note that each vowel has two forms - the marked version, and the unmarked version.

á: as in "Pa"   a: as in "ago"

é: as in "Hey"   e: as in "peck"

í: as in "Knee"   i: as in "pick"

ó: as in "Woe"   o: as in "mock"

ú: as in "Shoe"   u: as in "muck"

Again, though, I suggest bookmarking some YouTube videos of Irish Gaelic speakers and listening to the way the language rolls off their tongues. That will give you a sense of how the vowels and words

Here are a few phrases which you might want to practice, to get the feel of the Irish language and its rich sounds!

Welcome: Céad mile fáilte

Pleased to meet you: Tá áthas orm buaileadh leat

I am happy: Tá áthas orm

Yes: Ba mhaith liom

No: Níl

Thank You: taing dhut

Beautiful: àillidh

Beloved: caomh or gaolach

My Darling: a ghaoil

Love: gaol

My Love: a ghràidh or a luaidh

I love you: Ta gra agam ort

Will you marry me? An bpósfaidh tú mé?

Marriage: lanamnus

Always: a-chaoidh

Irish-Style Date Ideas

Whether you're just getting to know that special someone, are having a treasured night out after years together, or even kicking up your heels with friends, here are some suggestions to add the touch of the Irish to your next outing:

An Evening at the Pub

Each time we visit Ireland, one of the most classic activities for friends and family is to spend the evening at the local pub.

Note that this is *not* a sports bar where they all stare zombie-like at the TV screen! Rather, it's a social gathering with flowing drinks and live music. There's laughter, singing, and dancing. Often the party is still going hard when "last call" is sounded!

Get a bunch of your friends together, pour the beer, and laugh about whatever life has thrown at you.

Dance the Night Away

A sure-fire way to celebrate life the Irish way is to head out for a night of dancing. The Irish love to dance. Just about any festive occasion features music and dance.

Folk dancing would be great, if you have it available in your neighborhood, but any kind of dancing will get the Irish blood flowing in your feet.

Even dance around your own home to Irish music!

Darts

Ah, the classic hobby of choice in Ireland. Pretty much every local pub has a dart board or two on its walls. Newcomers are often welcomed to join in in a game or two.

Many Irish pubs have dart leagues, and folk come in from miles around to hang out with their friends and engage in some friendly competition.

It's a low impact sport that just about anyone can master.

Fishing

Head out on a fishing trip! Look in the closet of just about any Irish home, and you'll find the fishing supplies waiting for their next use. When Bob and I travel throughout Ireland, and stay at bed and breakfasts, often the owners encourage us to go out and fish for a while. They provide everything we need.

You can take a picnic lunch down to your local river, or head out for a day on a fishing boat. A lot of time fishing is spent just talking together and strengthening bonds, something any friendship or relationship could use!

Here's the fishing stream behind our family's cottage.

Horse Racing

The Irish adore racing. They often travel to get to a race and enjoy the afternoon as a grand adventure. One style of racing is a "point to point." They create a looped track in a meadow, including hurdles for the horses to leap over, and then everyone bets on which horse will win. The bets are closed and the horses take off! It's quite exciting.

Here's a photo from one of the point-to-points we attended in Mallow.

An Irish Proposal

Faigh do bhean i gcóngar, ach i bhfad uait díol do bhó

Get your wife locally, but far away from you sell your cow.

—Gaelic proverb

In Ireland, family is extremely important, and adult life was full of chores and tasks. It was assumed that an Irish boy or girl would marry when they reached seventeen or eighteen and would become a fully contributing member of the village. Irish lads and lasses would spend much of their childhood dreaming about their marriage and what they would do, and with whom they would be.

In Christian Ireland, a marriage was often arranged by the two fathers, who were seeking to enhance their land, livestock holdings, or rank. Heated discussions would be held about the number of cows on a property, the value of the land, and the quality of the crops grown there. Marriage was seen as an extremely religious and serious commitment that affected not only the families involved but the entire well-being of the village. Young adults saw marriage as a duty they must fulfill, and as a way they could give back to their family after being cared for, for so many years.

As couples in love sometimes tend to be rebellious, there were also a few cases of headstrong lovers that did not agree with their family's desires. A tradition existed for these young lovers to simply "run off" and get married somewhere, to defy what their parents felt was best for the family. The couple would get married, legally and properly, at a location outside the village. They would stay at that remote location to consummate the marriage and make it official and irrevocable. The new married pair would then return with the deed done, having avoided all of the pressure and parental influence normally expected, but still preparing for parental wrath.

There would of course be some unhappiness that the family fortunes had been harmed by this, and annoyance by the parents that their wishes had been circumvented. Still, there would also be the understanding that this path chosen by young lovers was part of the Irish tradition.

A proposal in Ireland could therefore come in two ways. On one hand, it could be the family-sanctified, father-arranged marriage that promotes the health and welfare of two families. Children were brought up to expect this case and to feel it was their responsibility to do their part to help out their family. On the other hand, it could be the impetuous love of two people who swear their hearts to one another, regardless of what family or friends think about it.

Ross Abbey, Roscrea

Engagement Bracelet

Many Irish were too poor to afford special rings for engagement. Gold bands would be a dream of riches beyond their imagining. Instead, an Irish tradition and sign of true love was of the Engagement Bracelet.

This bracelet was woven from the hair of the lovers. The woman would give the man a bracelet woven of her hair, and the man would reciprocate with one made from his own.

The bracelets were a truly unique gift, created from their own hair - a symbol of fertility and youth.

Rings

The more wealthy Irish would both give rings for the engagement phase and then at the wedding exchange bands of gold. Gold was the most precious metal available and has been a symbol of love and loyalty for centuries.

The Irish were and are great metalworkers. They can create beautiful jewelry with intricate Celtic designs.

Even in the days of Saint Brigid in the 600s, the Abbess had formed a great school of metalworking.

Gemstones

If the family had money, a precious stone would often be set into the engagement band. To make the ring unique and special for the woman who received it, the gem would often be her birthstone.

These would be:

January: Garnet
February: Amethyst
March: Bloodstone
April: Diamond
May: Emerald
June: Alexandrite
July: Ruby
August: Sardonyx
September: Sapphire
October: Tourmaline
November: Citrine
December: Lapis Lazuli

The gem could also be the color of the family into which she was marrying. It could even be set with two stones - one from her own family and one of her husband's.

The Claddagh Ring

A more recent option is the Claddagh ring. This is not actually an engagement ring - it is ring signifying "I am taken." Created in Galway Bay, the ring was given to the wife or fiancé who remained behind when their love went overseas, either to war or to seek a fortune. It was a sign to any men around that this woman was already spoken for and should not be flirted with.

The Claddagh ring originated in a small village near Galway, named "An Cladach" in Irish Gaelic, meaning a stony shore. It was very common across Europe for rings of friendship and love to incorporate a pair of hands and a heart. What the Claddagh added to this was the crown above – to show loyalty.

Here are two of my Claddagh rings, with my birthstone, the amethyst.

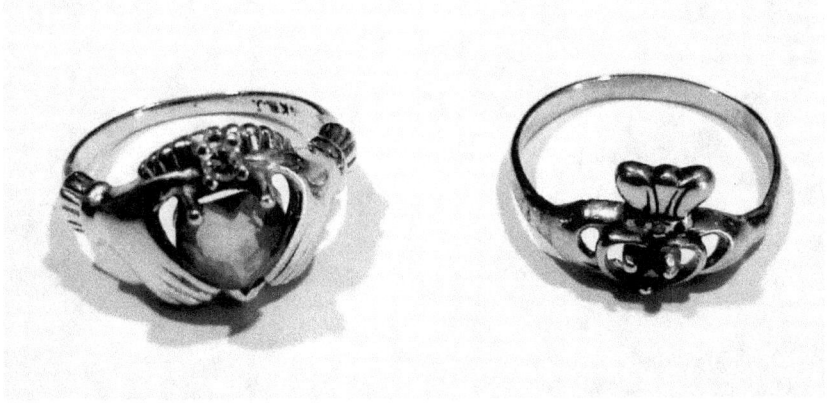

Many modern day couples who appreciate this symbolism have incorporated the Claddagh symbol into their own engagement or wedding bands.

A tradition in Europe is to put words around the inside of a ring, where they are closer to the wearer's heart, and private. The words might be the name of the couple, or an Irish Gaelic phrase. Here are a few appropriate choices:

Always: a-chaoidh

Beloved: caomh or gaolach

My Darling: a ghaoil

Love: gaol

I love you: Ta gra agam ort

Proposing the Irish Way

An bpósfaidh tú mé?

Will you marry me?

Many engagements in Ireland take place in the early part of the year, up until Ash Wednesday. Shrove Sunday, Shrove Monday and Shrove Tuesday would be a prime time for local villagers to tease any unmarried individuals and pressure them to take the plunge. The first Sunday in Lent was in fact called "Chalk Sunday". Young boys would run around with chalk and mark the backs of any single man to show that they should have been married by now.

Often around this time, local musicians would make up songs listing the names of unmarried men and women in the area, and sing it to the great glee of those listening. It helped encourage the people on the list to find a way to get off it quickly!

The traditional time for weddings in Ireland is in the fall or early winter, so an engagement at the beginning of the year gave the couple plenty of time to plan for the upcoming wedding.

Irish Engagement Traditions

With all of the traditions and rituals involved in choosing or finding a proper person to marry, it's no surprise that even more exist around the actual event itself! Just about every step of the process had its own rituals and rules to help ensure a long, happy marriage. Life in Ireland was not easy, and a new couple would want every extra bit of help that they could manage.

Here are many of the traditions that helped the Irish ensure a long, happy, fruitful marriage. They would hope for the luck of the leprechaun, the avoidance of the attention of the faeries, and the blessings of fertility and love. Share in the traditions, and bring great luck and love into your own relationship!

Choosing the Wedding Date

"God our Father, you sent Saint Patrick to preach your glory to the people of Ireland. By the help of his prayers, may all Christians proclaim your love to all men. Grant this through our Lord Jesus Christ, your Son, who lives and reigns with you and the Holy Spirit, one God, for ever and ever."

—Saint Patrick Prayer

Saint Patrick was the most venerated saint in Irish history, and until recently children were not even named Patrick because the name was sacred. Saint Patrick's saint day was considered one of the most holy days of the year, and March 17th was by far the most popular for an Irish couple to get married. Marriage was a religious ceremony, with serious vows, and to make this vow on Saint Patrick's Day was the ultimate promise.

Another very lucky day to wed was the last day of the year, December 31st. It was a way to enter a fresh, new year with a new partner by your side and a new outlook on life.

In comparison, it was extremely unlucky to marry on Christmas, as this should be a day dedicated to Christ alone. It was also unlucky to marry during Lent, which was a time for fasting, not feasting.

Each day of the week had its own saying:

Monday for health,

Tuesday for wealth,

Wednesday the best day of all,

Thursday for losses,

Friday for crosses and

Saturday no day at all.

Unlike other cultures, where marrying on Sunday was special because it meant there were two masses held, the Irish culture practically forbade a marriage on Sunday. They did not wish any of the revelry which would follow the wedding to take place on a holy day. The best days to marry were early in the week, so that there would be plenty of time to recover and clean up before the next church day rolled around again.

Irish traditions also provide a poem to help you choose which month to marry in:

Marry when the year is new, always loving, kind, and true.

When February birds do mate, you may wed, nor dread your fate.

If you wed when March winds blow, joy and sorrow both you'll know.

Marry in April when you can, joy for maiden and for man.

Marry in the month of May, you will surely rue the day.

Marry when June roses blow, over land and sea you'll go.

They who in July do wed, must labor always for their bread.

Whoever wed in August be, many a change are sure to see.

Marry in September's shine, your living will be rich and fine.

If in October you do marry, love will come but riches tarry.

If you wed in bleak November, only joy will come, remember.

When December's rain fall fast, marry and true love will last.

November was considered the most lucky month in which to marry. For the Irish, November was when all of the important summer and harvest work was complete, but the cold of winter had not yet arrived.

The Irish Wedding Invitation

For centuries, the Irish have been lauded for their beautiful work in calligraphy and illumination, or decorative writing. The Book of Kells is a great example of fine illumination. To add an Irish touch to your wedding invitation, look into using this same style of writing on your wedding invitation.

You can print your invitations on parchment, and use scrollwork or Celtic symbols on the sides. If you can afford it, there are even many people who will hand-calligraph your invitations. You could just have hand-calligraphy on the envelopes if doing the entire invitation is too costly.

Irish Wedding Poetry and Blessings

Ireland is a land of toasts, blessings, and sayings. Many combine the Irish reverence for their God with their innate sense of wit and humor. Any one of these blessings might be perfect for inclusion on your wedding invitation, in your wedding ceremony as a theme for a party, or as a toast during any Irish-themed dinner.

May the road rise to meet you.

May the wind be always at your back.

May the sun shine warm upon your face.

And rains fall soft upon your fields.

And until we meet again,

May God hold you in the hollow of His hand.

♡ ♡ ♡

May the Lord keep you in His hand

And never close His fist too tight.

♡ ♡ ♡

May you always have work for your hands to do.

May your pockets hold always a coin or two.

May the sun shine bright on your windowpane.

May the rainbow be certain to follow each rain.

May the hand of a friend always be near you.

And may God fill your heart with gladness to cheer you.

♡ ♡ ♡

May God be with you and bless you,

May you see your children's children,

May you be poor in misfortune, rich in blessings.

May you know nothing but happiness

From this day forward.

♡ ♡ ♡

Always remember to forget

The things that made you sad.

But never forget to remember

The things that made you glad.

Always remember to forget

The friends that proved untrue.

But never forget to remember

Those that have stuck by you.

Always remember to forget

The troubles that passed away.

But never forget to remember

The blessings that come each day.

♡ ♡ ♡

May the saddest day of your future be no worse

Than the happiest day of your past.

♡ ♡ ♡

May there be a generation of children

On the children of your children.

♡ ♡ ♡

May you live to be a hundred years,

With one extra year to repent!

♡ ♡ ♡

May your neighbors respect you,

Trouble neglect you,

The angels protect you,

And heaven accept you.

♡ ♡ ♡

May the Irish hills caress you.

May her lakes and rivers bless you.

May the luck of the Irish enfold you.

May the blessings of Saint Patrick behold you.

♡ ♡ ♡

May your pockets be heavy and your heart be light,

May good luck pursue you each morning and night.

♡ ♡ ♡

Walls for the wind,

And a roof for the rain,

And drinks beside the fire –

Laughter to cheer you

And those you love near you,

And all that your heart may desire!

♡ ♡ ♡

May God grant you many years to live,

For sure He must be knowing

The earth has angels all too few

And heaven is overflowing.

♡ ♡ ♡

May peace and plenty be the first

To lift the latch to your door,

And happiness be guided to your home

By the candle of Christmas.

♡ ♡ ♡

May you always have these blessings:

A soft breeze when summer comes,

A warm fireside in winter,

And always the warm, soft smile of a friend.

The Night Before the Wedding

Your plans for the night before the wedding may depend on whether you follow the new, Christian traditions, or the older, Celtic traditions.

In the Christian tradition, a wedding was a serious affair. It was a permanent vow being made before God. Often it was being made between two individuals who barely knew each other, at the order of their fathers to create a land deal. The Christian wedding adherents would often pray the evening before for prosperity and children, and for a partner they could learn to care for. They would both be happy that they were doing the right thing for themselves and their families, and determined to put in the work required to make the marriage successful. The two would then go to sleep early, to be sure they were as ready as possible for this great step in their lives.

However, for those who follow the more Celtic route, a wedding was a step towards childbearing, a ceremony to celebrate fertility. It was a union being made between two individuals who had perhaps already gone through a year of handfasting, who perhaps even were living together already as lovers, and who enjoyed the thought of having children together. It was a celebration of new life more than the tying together of two families.

Some of the more secluded areas of Ireland still celebrate the fertility aspect of the ceremony. In Leitrim and Mayo especially, there is the night-before tradition of the "straw boys." A group of nine boys arrive in straw masks and outfits. They should not be recognized, and they dance with the bride-to-be and her friends. They celebrate her fertility and health. The straw boys are of course her groom-to-be and his friends, and the dancing help them to celebrate that they, like many couples before and to come, are part of the eternal cycle of fertility and life. The night was a special one, for the bride to be and groom to be to share together.

An Irish Wedding

"Do not torment me, lady Let our purposes agree
You are my spouse on this Fair Plain so let us embrace."
— old Irish poem

Finally, the much-anticipated wedding day has arrived. With an engagement happening in the early spring, and the wedding normally happening in the late fall, the wedding day would come after many months of planning and preparation. The bride and groom were both very nervous, but also eager to go through with the ceremony and move on to their married life and their new places in the village.

To the Celtic culture, a wedding was a time to celebrate and dance! A pair of people who had been in the village for years, and had perhaps been lovers for a while, had now chosen willingly to bring children into the community. This was a cause for great festivities and many fertility offerings.

To the Irish Christians, a wedding was a time to bear witness to a formal vow before God. It was a lifelong commitment, not only between two individuals, but also the permanent joining of two families. It would change the ownership of land and cattle, and could affect the financial well-being of the entire village.

For both the Celts and the Christians, a wedding was a time of feasting and plenty. Even in hard times, a wedding was a chance to eat delicious food, drink gallons of whiskey and beer, and dance and sing until the sun rose in the morning!

Getting to the Church

The early Irish would be married at a sacred site, or simply exchange vows at the home. For the later Christian Irish, a wedding ceremony wasn't just a 'nice gathering at a church'. These Irish were extremely religious, and a wedding mass was a full mass, with extra time spent on the couple as well.

Most Irish families were not rich enough to afford a wagon or steed. The groom's family would walk with him to the local village church first, and his best man would stand by his side. The two would wait at the altar for the bride to arrive while the guests were seated. I've been at Irish weddings where the groom waited there for more than an hour, nervously wondering if she would appear!

The bride would then walk to the church with her family as escort. Often the local villagers would hand the family presents as they passed, either pans or cutlery or other useful items.

If a funeral was going on at the same time, the route the wedding party walked would be planned to ensure it did not intercept that of the funeral. This was both to keep the wedding cheerful and not to further upset the grieving of the funeral.

A horse and carriage was a lovely way for the more wealthy bride to make a traditional entrance. The horse and carriage would both be decorated with flowers which matched her chosen bouquet.

Whatever way the bride got to the church, she would wait until all were seated and ready before she made her entrance. For a Christian wedding, the bride's father had responsibility of the maiden until this point. He was then handing ownership of the bride and all of her possessions and dowry over to the groom's care. The bride's father would therefore walk her down the aisle, and then place her hand in the groom's firm, waiting one.

Church Ceremony

The wedding ceremony for an Irish church wedding was a solemn, religious full mass. An extra set of ceremony was added on for the wedding, but the core of the ceremony was the full religious mass. The ceremony would *not* be held on a Sunday. It could be on any other day, and Wednesday was the luckiest day to choose.

The bride would traditionally stand to the left of the groom. In the days of swords and ruffians, this would allow the groom to keep his sword hand free in case of trouble.

A full Irish wedding was an endurance event, which is why the celebration afterwards often went on for days.

A lovely aspect of some Irish weddings is the "ring warming." The wedding rings would be passed around the church from hand to hand. Each witness would hold the rings for a moment and send their fond thoughts and prayers to the bride and groom.

Handfasting

For those with a non-Catholic background, the other option is the pre-church tradition of handfasting.

The Irish come from a society with an ancient history. They realized how difficult it could be for two people, while dating, to *truly* know if they were meant to live together for the rest of their lives. They believed in having lovers, marrying when children were involved, and separating if things did not work out. As Christianity came in, they began to feel that once a couple was officially married, they should stay together until death.

To resolve these two different points of view, they developed the practice of "Handfasting." In a sense, handfasting was a trial marriage, which lasted for a year and a day. Instead of being tied by a full religious ceremony, a handfasting was more of a personal commitment, made by the local lord with a ribbon that tied the two hands together. This is where the term "tying the knot" comes from in modern days.

The handfasting ceremony was both simple and meaningful. The two would commit to try their very best to make the relationship work for that year. They would give it their full attention and be true to each other. However, they also understood that some people simply don't get along well, and that this is what the period of time was to determine.

If, at the end of the year, the couple was still content, they would go on to the full, permanent, religious ceremony. However, if the couple found that, despite their best efforts, they simply did not live well together, they would depart as friends, with much learned wisdom from the time, and look for someone better matched.

The Bride

As in pretty much every culture from the beginning of time, a bride often seeks to look her very best on her wedding day. This is her day to celebrate before friends and family the love she shares for another person. All eyes will be on her. She wants to glow

Here are traditions that have been treasured in Ireland for centuries.

Wedding Dress

The national color of Ireland was blue until very recently, and blue is also the traditional color of purity. It was only in the 1700s that white became associated with purity - before then white stood for both joy and death.

Because of those reasons, the Irish wedding dress was often blue in color.

As much as Ireland is covered in green, green tended to be avoided at weddings. It was thought to lure in nature-loving faeries who would then cause mischief.

The bride's dress was usually not a special dress bought for the purpose - that would have seemed unnecessarily frivolous to the practical Irish! Still, the bride's best dress would be decorated with extra embroidery, lace, and silk.

If the bride could afford a silk dress, this was the most sought-after choice. Celtic designs would be woven into it.

Singerleens

Again, because the traditional wedding dress would simply be the bride's best dress "livened up" for this special occasion, the family and friends would see out ways to enliven it.

One such effort was done with singerleens. These were small pieces of jewelry which would be attached to the dress.

Many cultures celebrate horses and horseshoes as signs of luck. It's no wonder, with how critical a strong horse could be to the survival of a family in these times. Rather than carry an entire horseshoe with her, a bride would often have a singerleen in the shape of an up-turned horseshoe. That way all the luck would catch within it and bless her new life.

Handkerchief

Until fairly recently it was quite common for both men and women to carry handkerchiefs with them. They could be used for a variety of practical purposes.

The bride would have a white handkerchief with her during the wedding for all of those reasons – to dab at tears of joy and to wipe away any food spills. She would then keep that handkerchief, and sew it into a bonnet for her child's wedding.

If that child is a girl, that girl can then use the same handkerchief, back in its original form, for her own wedding.

The Wedding Cloak

To keep her warm on those misty Irish mornings, the bride would often wear a bright red cloak. This showed her love and also made it easy for the groom to keep an eye on her!

If you're looking into buying a cloak, I highly recommend you get one that ends a few inches off the ground. I know it looks romantic to have the cloak sweeping the ground behind you – but this gets impractical extremely quickly. There's a reason that, in the days of cloak-wearing, most people wore cloaks that stayed up off the dirt.

Veils

Irish brides would wear a veil to protect her against jealous faeries and their pranks. Also, as some Irish marriages were arranged between the groom's father and the bride's father, the bride was at times not known to the groom. The veil helped shield her features from him, to supposedly keep him from running off before the ceremony was complete.

Tradition has it that a happily married woman should be the one to put the veil on the bride before the ceremony.

Hair and Headwear

While courting, maidens would wear their long hair loose. But a bride would wish for something more special. A special headdress would have seemed ostentatious to the practical Irish. Instead, the bride would braid her long hair into intricate patterns.

Most Irish brides would wear wildflowers in their hair, either lavender or other local plants of which they were fond.

Sometimes the bride would weave a wreath for their head. This would also contain herbs, to help protect her from the attention of faeries and to bring her luck and fertility.

Myrtle

One of the key Irish herbs for romance is Myrtle. This was an herb
which brought luck and love to Irish brides. An Irish bride would
carry myrtle until the wedding was done. She would then give some
of the myrtle to each of her bridesmaids, to bring them romance of
their own.

The Groom

The fairies and leprechauns had to be kept at bay during the ceremony, so they did not cause mischief. The bridegroom would keep one button on his right knee undone, to help ensure that the fairies could not cause him any harm. The faeries would think he was not finished dressing, and would not know the wedding was taking place.

The groom would also grow out his beard for the weeks leading up to the wedding. The full growth of beard was a visible sign of his virility.

The groom waited by the altar for his bride to come to him, and received responsibility for the bride from her father. He then stood to her right during the long formal mass and ceremony.

When the ceremony was over, the groom kissed the bride. He then escorted his new wife out of the church and into their new world as man and wife.

The New Coin

During the ceremony, after the rings have been blessed by the priest, this is traditionally the moment where the groom presents the bride with a brand new coin.

He says to her:

"I give you this gold and silver as a token of all I possess."

This mirrors what Peter says in Acts 3:6:

"I don't have any silver or gold for you. But I'll give you what I have."

In essence the groom is vowing to share his full life and prosperity with his new partner. The Biblical scene is where a poor man is healed and made whole again.

The coin is then saved by the bride, to be given to her eldest son for him to give to his own bride.

After the Ceremony

While many cultures end a wedding with a smashed glass, to symbolize their new lives together, Irish tradition says that a broken glass on a wedding day brings bad luck. An Irish couple planning their wedding might want to find a pair of pewter goblets for sharing a toast.

When the new couple emerged from the wedding, the church bells would ring loudly to scare off any lurking faeries or evil spirits. In early days, the local lads would fire rifles into the air in celebration, but in modern times car horns are used.

Often, to bring fertility to the couple, rice would be thrown as they walked. There are current myths that imply rice expands in the bellies of birds and harms the birds, and shouldn't be used. This is quite untrue - rice is harmless to birds! Traditionally minded couples should not worry about scattering rice.

For wealthier couples, the groom would toss a handful of coins in the air, to share his new-found wealth with family and friends. This tradition was known as "The Grushie" and was primarily done by noble families who had that wealth to spare. Of course, if you're going to be throwing anything at the people in attendance, be sure to warn them first! You could get someone in the eyeball otherwise.

An Irish Reception

The Irish are enormous fans of any celebration involving delicious food, ample drink, festive music, and lots of dancing. Food and drink were expected to overflow from the end of the ceremony into the next day and beyond. It was not uncommon for breakfast to be served the next morning to whoever still remained awake after a night of dancing and singing.

Many wedding invitations in Ireland specify the times for the various stages of the evening. That way, guests who might not wish to attend the long religious ceremony could simply join the festivities afterwards.

Read up on the traditions surrounding an Irish wedding reception, and incorporate some touches into your own!

Traditions for a Happy Marriage

Every culture has its traditions about what helps a couple find continual happiness. Ireland has a great folklore of leprechauns and fairies, and it is no surprise that one of the key fears during a reception is that fairies will come and run off with the happy celebrants. Jokes are often made about this during wedding receptions.

Women are thought of as jealous creatures, and because of that, a man should be the first to wish joy to the new bride.

If the day was rainy, it meant hard times for the new couple. This is a cruel tradition to have in a land as rainy as Ireland! On the other hand, a sunny day meant they would have many happy years ahead.

Birds are an integral part of the Irish landscape. It is very lucky for the new couple to hear the cry of a cuckoo or a magpie after the ceremony.

Food and drink both figured strongly in an Irish relationship. The floor of the reception area would be sprinkled with whiskey, to bring good luck to the new couple.

In some areas of Ireland, the new groom would go with his bride to an area that had a mill, stream, and a tree nearby. These were all symbols of fertility and long life. The bride would give him fresh butter on a newly made dish to symbolize the products of her home and the food she would provide to the family.

The groom would then whisper:

"Oh, woman, loved by me, mayest thou give me
thy heart, thy soul, and thy body."

For those who favored drink, a bride would take a glass of wine or beer that she was to serve to her groom. She would then say over it, three times:

> "This is the charm I set for love:
> A woman's charm of love and desire;
> you for me and I for thee and for none else;
> your face to mine and your hand turned away from all others."

Decorations and Flowers

Faeries love the color green, and it attracts their attention. It is considered very bad luck to have green clothing on during a wedding reception, for it will catch the eye of the faeries, who will come and cause trouble.

If it's an Irish theme you're hoping for, go for blue and gold. These were the traditional colors of Ireland for many years, and blue is the color of St. Patrick. You can also go with the colors of the bride's family and groom's family

For any religious ceremony, the shape of a shamrock would be a perfect symbol. The shamrock was used by St. Patrick to explain the meaning of the trinity to the early Irish. Just avoid it in green – gold and white are lovely colors to use.

Roses are a symbol of love in just about every culture, and this is especially true in Ireland. You can decorate the reception hall with climbing roses, and incorporate roses into the bridal bouquet.

Another common wedding plant is the foxglove. For the Irish, it symbolizes the innocence and dreams of youth.

Consider decorating the head table with The Bells of Ireland. These flowers are thought to bring the luck of the Irish, and are traditionally given when people start a new endeavor.

The Irish love pastel colors, and heather is one of their favorite flowers. The Irish associate colored heather with various benefits. These are:

Pink heather for luck
Purple heather for passion
White heather for a safe home.

Use bouquets of all three heather colors to triply-bless the new couple.

Note that there are two flowers to stay away from during a reception. These are the lilac and apple blossom. Both are associated with sorrow and bad luck.

Irish Music and Dance

The Irish are enthusiastic fans of music and dance. Head out to any Irish pub as the sun sets and you will find a group of musicians playing away, with people singing, dancing, and enjoying the music well into the wee hours. The social life in Ireland often revolves around the pub.

An Irish wedding is like an extended celebration. While the ceremony is religious, and the meal is formal, the dancing and singing can go on until the following morning. Often, when invitations are issued, the expectation is that a number of people may bypass the ceremony and dinner, and show up for the evening of celebration.

A nice touch during the ceremony and dinner is to have a harper play. The harper is one of the oldest traditions in Ireland, and the harp is the national symbol of Ireland. The blue and gold flag of Ireland until the 1800s showed a harp on a field of blue. There are many, many beautiful Celtic harp pieces that would make a wonderful accompaniment for a wedding ceremony or meal.

Another Irish tradition is the Uilleann pipes. Where Scottish bagpipes were made to play war tunes during a battle, the Irish pipes are designed for dance tunes at a pub. If you can find a band with a good piper in it, you're guaranteed a grand time, at least until the last guests collapse from exhaustion!

Some weddings bring in trained Irish set dancers to perform during the reception. While this is a sweet idea, when this was done at a wedding in Ireland that I attended, the Irish people there were quite upset. They didn't want to *watch* dancers, they wanted to BE the dancers! To them, a party is about actively singing, dancing, and having fun. They appreciated the skill of the performers, but to them a wedding is about participating. They were very happy when the dancers left and the guests could take the floor to have fun.

A good alternative might be to have professional dancers come, and help teach the guests how to do set dances! That would allow those who already know the dance to enjoy the music, and help others become a part of the Irish tradition.

Here is a harp song by Shirley Starke, who runs Valkyrie Publications. Her music is available at bookstores and on her website, listed in the website reference area at the end of this book.

Your Heart Is As the Sunshine Warm by Shirley Starke

Your heart is as the sunshine warm;
Your smile is bright as day;
Your voice is sweet as an angel's song;
Your eyes are as the twilight grey.
There is beneath my joy in you
And your tenderness for me
A great love spreading out of sight
Like the roots of a mighty tree.
In a meadow dark with trees, Out of reach of my song,
Sure I held you under the stars
And kissed you tenderly, softly, and long.
A life is like a standing pier,
And time is like a river;
Our souls are leaves that ride the stream,
And love goes on forever.
Some day, before our lives are done,
I pray to God it will be:
Our love will rise like a swelling tide
And sweep, and sweep us both to sea.
Then in a meadow dark with trees,
Beyond the reach of my song,
I'll hold you there beneath the stars
And kiss you tenderly, softly, and long.

An Irish Wedding Cake

Bread is always a symbol of fertility, and this was a focus in wedding ceremonies. In the Roman days, cakes were broken over the head of the new wife for luck, to make her fertile. Guests would gather up the crumbs to share in that luck.

As time went on, the tradition changed so that a large wedding cake was presented to all of the guests, so that sharing fertility was a bit easier, and neater!

Ireland is a land of farmers and practical people. To them a wedding cake is not about a fanciful spun sugar creation. Rather, it is about a rich, hearty fruit cake that is filling and delicious.

Often, the top layer of the cake would be a special whiskey cake. This would be set aside by the bride and groom and frozen until their first-born child was christened. Similarly, a slice of the wedding cake itself was to be saved and eaten on the first wedding anniversary.

Here is a recipe for a traditional Irish wedding cake.

70 oz glace cherries
1 lb golden raisins
9 oz raisins
1 lb currants
7 oz shredded almonds
1 Tbsp flour
1 lb flour
1 tsp salt
1 tsp nutmeg
1 tsp cinnamon
1 lb butter
1 lb brown sugar
2 Tbsp molasses
1 tsp orange zest
1 tsp lemon zest
1 ½ tsp vanilla extract
8 large eggs

4 Tbsp brandy

Mix together the cherries, both types of raisins, currants, and almonds. Mix in a tablespoon of flour. Sift the rest of the flour with the salt, nutmeg, and cinnamon.

Separately, blend the butter and sugar. Mix in the molasses, orange zest, lemon zest, and vanilla. Slowly mix in the eggs, then add in the flour mixture. Finally, blend in the fruit and brandy.

Grease a large cake pan and pour in the cake batter. Bake the cake at 300°F (150°C) for 1 1/2 hrs. Reduce heat to 275°F (135°C) and cook for another 3 hours, or until a toothpick inserted in the center comes out clean. Poke holes into the cake with a fork and pour in additional brandy to taste.

Traditional Wedding Presents

Again, with the Irish being a practical people, wedding gifts were usually things that the couple could use in their new life together. Clothes. Household items.

One traditional gift in Ireland was bells. The bells were said to remind the couple of their wedding vows, in the coming years of life together.

After the Reception

An Irish wedding reception could easily last until the sun rose the following morning. Coffee might be poured and a full Irish breakfast enjoyed by those who lasted the night! At some point, however, the new couple would need to make their way to their new home together, looking forward to sharing their marriage bed.

The freshly married couple would be sure to choose a new route to their home, to show that they had now chosen a new path in life together. They would also be sure to take the longest road possible, to enjoy their quiet time together before they entered their new land of chores and tasks.

When the two reached their home, the husband would carry his wife over the threshold. In part this was to evade the mischievous leprechauns that lingered there, hoping to trip the bride as she entered her new home. Also, the action of carrying the bride is a throwback to the days of family wars. In those days, warring Irish men would simply 'capture' the women they wished to marry from an opposing clan and drag them back home again.

Most Irish couples could not afford to leave the farm to take a honeymoon — the land and animals needed their constant attention. Also, they often did not have the money to afford such a trip. Instead, they would celebrate their 'new month' at home, enjoying their time together and settling into their new life.

Irish Toasts

"Better belly burst than good liquor be lost."
—Jonathan Swift

The Irish pub is the center of Irish social life. Whole families head to the pub after work to chat with friends, watch the latest news, discuss politics, sing along with local musicians, and dance. The traditional drink is a pint of beer, and the pints keep flowing until the wee hours of the morning! It is rude to refuse to be part of a round, so usually those who can't keep up switch to something smaller or less potent. Bailey's Irish Cream is a good substitution since it is served in very small glasses with a great deal of ice!

The traditional Irish toast is Sláinte! This is Irish Gaelic for "To your health!" To pronounce it, slur the words "It's a lawn chair!"

Here are some other classic Irish toasts. The Irish have a keen sense of humor, and combined with their love of a good drink, there are thousands of toasts floating around this island:

May the roof above us never fall in,

And may we friends gathered below never fall out.

♡ ♡ ♡

May your glass be ever full.

May the roof over your head be always strong.

And may you be in heaven

Half an hour before the devil knows you're dead.

♡ ♡ ♡

Here's to me, and here's to you,

And here's to love and laughter-

I'll be true as long as you,

And not one moment after.

♡ ♡ ♡

Here's to you and yours

And to mine and ours.

And if mine and ours

Ever come across to you and yours,

I hope you and yours will do

As much for mine and ours

As mine and ours have done

For you and yours!

♡ ♡ ♡

Health and life to you;

The mate of your choice to you;

Land without rent to you,

And death in Eirinn.

♡ ♡ ♡

Here's a toast to your enemies' enemies!

♡ ♡ ♡

When we drink, we get drunk.

When we get drunk, we fall asleep.

When we fall asleep, we commit no sin.

When we commit no sin, we go to heaven.

So, let's all get drunk, and go to heaven!

♡ ♡ ♡

Here's to a long life and a merry one.

A quick death and an easy one.

A pretty girl and an honest one.

A cold beer - and another one!

Clinking of Wine Glasses and Toasts

As with many of our food traditions, the clinking of glasses traces its root to the health and safety of the drinker. In this case, it goes back to the tendency of nobles to kill each other off by poisoning their food!

Wine was very commonly drunk during medieval days because it was one of the only safe liquids available. Water was often polluted, and milk was both useful for other things and thought to be for children only. As the wine was often full of sediment, a poison was easily introduced into it.

To prove that his wine was safe, the host would pour a bit of his guest's wine into his own glass and drink it first, to prove it was safe. If the guest trusted his host, however, he would merely clink his flagon against that of his host's when his host offered his cup for the sample. The 'clink' (or perhaps 'clunk' back then, since wood or metal was more common for drinking vessels) was a sign of trust and honesty.

Later, as metal and glass became more common, the chiming noise also brought a festive feel to events, and brought to mind the 'safe' feeling of church bells.

Irish Drinks

"Let schoolmasters puzzle their brain
with grammar, and nonsense, and learning.
Good liquor, I stoutly maintain
Gives genius a better discerning."
—Oliver Goldsmith

The Irish are firm believers in the power of good alcohol. They rarely drink wine, and instead enjoy their fine pints of Guinness and the other, stronger liquors that keep them warm on a cold winter's night.

Here are some of the traditional Irish drinks that would be served at any special occasion.

Irish Whiskey

One of the most famous drinks of Ireland is Irish Whiskey.
Whiskey is a hard liquor produced by distilling malted barley into a
fermented beverage. Monks first brought the technique of
distillation back to Ireland in the 500s, after traveling to other
countries where the process had been discovered.

Over the centuries, the Irish perfected the technique, and refined it
with their own native ingredients. The word "Whiskey" comes from
the Irish word "usquebaugh", meaning "water of life". Religious
orders were especially fond of the drink for its many medicinal
and antiseptic uses. By the late 1400s, records indicate it was also
called "aquavitae" which means "water of life" in Latin. Note that
the Irish and Americans use the "whiskey" spelling, while the
Scottish and Canadians tend to use the word "whisky" without the
"e".

In early years, whiskey was thick and smoky, mostly because the
malt was dried by rich peat fires in between distillation runs.
However, when a continual still was invented in the early 1800s,
the whiskey became lighter and smoother, and much more
popular.

Bushmills

Bushmills is the oldest legal distillery in Ireland, formed in the 1600s and still running strong today. It prides itself on smooth whiskeys, created by drying the malted barley in closed ovens. This shields it from the smoke and lets its natural flavor shine through. Bushmills also triple-distills its whiskey to bring out more of the pure flavor. The Bushmills distillery is open for visits. It is conveniently located near the Giant's Causeway, an amazing natural formation found on the north coast of Ireland.

Ballylarkin

Ballylarkin Liqueur is a blended, flavored whiskey. It combines Irish whiskey with flavors of vanilla and citrus. Most people drink it warm, as a cordial.

Baileys Irish Cream

Baileys is actually a recent invention. For decades, Englishmen had been drinking a mixture of Scotch and milk to help with ulcers. The problem in pre-mixing this concoction was that soon it would curdle into a clump that could only be used as an anchor. Baileys' biggest obstacle during development was to find stabilizing ingredients which would allow the drink to keep its great taste, but also help it stay creamy and smooth for a length of time.

The stabilizers they created are, of course, a Big Secret. All we know for sure is that Baileys blends fresh dairy cream, Irish whiskey, other spirits, and natural flavors, including chocolate and coffee. The cream accounts for 50% of the final volume of Baileys, while the whiskey used in Baileys is a triple-distilled Irish pot still whiskey (Scotch whisky is normally double-distilled).

A pot still is the most basic type of still - it is a still that is heated directly. The vapors from the alcohol move up into a coil, condense, and are collected.

This magical combination was hit upon in 1974, and from that small start Bailey's now uses 1/3 the total manufacturing milk in Ireland!

Baileys, with its Irish charm, was a hit in all lands. There are now 1,000 glasses of Baileys drunk every minute of every day. Baileys is sold in 130 countries. Compare this to Sutter Home White Zinfandel, perhaps the most popular wine on the planet, which fills a mere 432 glasses a minute.

How do you best care for your 'Irish milk'? First off, don't refrigerate it! Refrigeration affects the taste and is highly discouraged by the makers. On the other hand, Baileys contains no preservatives or additives and so should be consumed within 6 months of opening the bottle. What a dilemma! The attached recipes should help with this. Sláinte!

Bailey's Irish Flag Drink

1/3 shot green Creme de Menthe
1/3 shot Bailey's
1/3 shot Grand Marnier

Start with the green Creme de Menthe. Then slowly add in the Bailey's, pouring down the side of the glass or over a spoon so it doesn't mix in. When that layer is in, do the same thing to gently add the Grand Marnier. It looks fantastic and is perfect for parties!

Baileys Bomber

This easy Bailey's layered drink is created with Baileys and Scotch.

3/4oz Baileys Irish cream
1/4oz Scotch

In a clear glass, pour the Baileys in first. Then layer the Scotch over it gently by pouring down the bulge of an upside-down spoon.

B52 Layered Drink

Baileys Irish cream
Kahlua
Grand Marnier

This layered drink uses Kahlua, Baileys, and Grand Marnier. You can use them in a 1:1:1 ratio, or come up with your own ratio that both looks pretty and tastes delicious based on which of the three flavors you enjoy the most.

Pour the Kahlua into a clear glass. Now using an upside down spoon, pour the Baileys gently over the spoon so it fans out against the inside of the glass, drizzling gently on top of the Kahlua. It will form a second layer. Do the same with the Grand Marnier for the top layer. Enjoy!

Eggnog with Baileys Irish Cream

Want some Eggnog with an Irish heritage? Eggnog was enjoyed in Ireland back in the 1800s, and as soon as Baileys came out, this became a classic hit!

12 eggs
1 cup sugar
cup milk
cups Baileys Irish Cream
6 cups heavy cream
freshly grated nutmeg

In a large bowl, beat the eggs until very thick and creamy. Gradually beat in the sugar. Blend in the milk and the Baileys.

Whip the cream in another bowl until it holds soft peaks. Stir the whipped cream into the egg mixture. Chill until ready to serve.

When ready to serve, stir again and ladle into punch cups. Top each serving with a dusting of nutmeg.

Grasshopper

As you might guess, I love Bailey's Irish Cream. It's smooth and delicious tasting. This great recipe contains not only Bailey's, but also Godiva chocolate liqueur and creme de menthe. It's named a Grasshopper after the classic drink combination of cocoa, mint and cream with a whiskey base.

2oz Baileys Irish Cream
1/2oz Godiva Chocolate Liqueur
1/2oz Creme de Menthe

Shake all three ingredients together with ice. Serve over ice in a short glass. Enjoy!

Irish Honeymoons

" 'Tis never too late for delight, my dear;

And the best of all ways

To lengthen our days

Is to steal a few hours from the night, my dear!"

—Thomas Moore, Irish poet

oneymoon is a term invented by the Celts, and it refers literally to a month of honey. The newly married couple would spend their first month enjoying the fine taste of mead, drinking it to enhance their fertility and bring them many children!

Mead is a honey wine, with origins obscured in the mists of time. It is considered by many to be the first alcoholic beverage created, predating both grape wine and beer. It was mentioned in the epic Beowulf and was known to the Greeks and Romans.

Mead is perhaps best known as the drink of the Celts and Vikings, beloved by medieval re-enactors everywhere as an authentic drink of the times.

There are various styles of mead:

Cyser: Mead with apples or grape juice added

Hippocras: Mead with grape juice and spices

Metheglin: Mead with cloves, cinnamon, or other spices

Melomel: Mead with fruit juices and perhaps spices

Pyment: Mead with grape juice added

Sack: Extra-honey meads (note this term also applies to Sherry!)
Traditional: simply honey, water, and yeast

Mead is generally a light, fruity drink, light yellow in color. It should
be drunk very soon after purchase, and tends to do well as a mulled
wine or marinade, as well as a dessert wine.

Note that authentic mead does not involve grapes or white wine. It is
made solely by fermenting honey. Most wine shops carry a mead or
two, so give some a try!

Dandelion Wine

A traditional wine in Ireland is Dandelion Wine. This would be made each spring when the dandelions were in bloom, and drunk either on the Winter solstice or the following May Day. Make some while you're engaged, and drink the fruits of your labor during your wedding reception!

4 quarts dandelion heads
2 gallons water
3 lemons
3 large oranges
2 lb white sugar
2 lb dark brown sugar
12 oz clover honey
2 lb golden raisins
1 package yeast
1 piece bread, toasted

Pick the dandelions at mid-day when the blooms are wide open. Completely remove the stalks and leaves, but it is fine to leave on the little green under-petals. Put the flowers into a ceramic bowl. Boil the water, and pour it into the bowl over the flowers. Cover the bowl tightly with plastic wrap.

Let the mixture sit for 2 days, being sure to remove the plastic and stir it twice each day. Put the mix into a pot and bring it to a boil again. Peel the oranges and lemons and then break the peels up into large pieces. Into the pot, add the sugar, honey, lemon peels and orange peels. Boil for an hour. Return the mix to the ceramic bowl and add in the juice and the pulp of the lemons and oranges. Let the mixture stand until cool. Spread the yeast onto the toast, and then place the piece of toast on the top of the liquid, floating. Cover the container, and let it stand for 3 days.

Strain the mixture and put the liquid into a fermentation vessel – glass is preferred. Add in raisins and top with an airlock – something that lets extra air out, but doesn't let air in easily. Leave the blend to ferment until any bubbling stops. Then rack out the sediment and bottle the wine.

Dandelion wine is drinkable after 6 months, but tastes best after a year of aging.

I love making dandelion wine each spring. Just make sure not to use any pesticides on your lawn!

Living and Loving the Irish Way

E njoying the Irish way of life isn't about one ceremony or one moment. It's about treasuring each day that comes along, looking for the fun and joy that it can bring.

Yes, there are sorrows in life. The Irish have known years of work and toil, with rainy weeks and finger-numbing work. Through it all, they enjoy the times of sunshine, and take pride in the achievements of the day.

Find the luck of the Irish in your own life!

Irish Touches for your Life

Here are some Irish touches to bring to your own world.

Lucky Horseshoe

Many Irish traditions involve luck. In Ireland, it is very common to find an old horseshoe hung on a wall for luck. It should be turned so the ends point up. This ensures the luck doesn't run out.

St. Brigid's Cross

Saint Brigid is the patron saint of Ireland, and many Irish homes have a St. Brigid's Cross in at least one room.

Family Arms

Family was very important to the Irish. Research your own family's coat of arms, and those of your partner. Many shops sell color reproductions of your arms to hang with pride.

An Irish Garden

The Irish love their gardens and flowers! Fill yours with climbing roses, heather, foxglove and Irish bells. Add in your favorite herbs, especially myrtle, and surround it all with ivy.

Hobbies

There are many traditional Irish hobbies that you can enjoy as well. Probably the two greatest hobbies are music and singing, in any and all forms. An evening at home can involve a sing-along, and a gathering of friends is sure to lead to music and dance. Bring more music into your own life - especially Irish folk tunes - to share in that love.

Darts is a game loved by many Irish – probably because it can be played in a pub! Head down to most pubs on a cold wintry evening, and you're likely to find the darts flying in a friendly game. If you visit Ireland, carry a set of darts along with you! You'll easily meet new friends and be welcomed into the fun.

Fishing is both a hobby and a way of life for many Irish. From the lads that fish in the streams on the way to school to the men who fish the ocean for a living, fish hold a special place in the hearts of the Irish. Some of the finest fishing in the world can be found on the shores and waters of Ireland.

Ireland is well known for its fine embroidery and knitting, from warm Aran sweaters to beautifully done Celtic designs on dresses. If your skills tend towards needlework, look into decorating your world and clothing with an Irish flair.

Names and their Meanings

Is there a new child, a new pet, or even a new boat or plane in your life? An Irish name might be the perfect thing to bring luck and long life. Here are some traditional Irish names from which to choose.

Aidan (M): Fire

Ahern (M): Lord of the horses

Aine (F): Intelligence, glory

Alan (M): Peaceful, handsome

Angus (M): Strength, chosen one.

Binne (F): Sweet, gentle

Blathmac (M): Flower.

Blathmac was the name of a famous poet.

Brenda (F): Raven

Brendan (M): Prince

Brenna (F): Dark haired maiden

Brian (M): Noble

Bridget (F): Resolutely strong. There are many spellings of
Bridget, including Brigid & Brigette.

Brian (M): Strong

Brianna (F): Strong

Casey (M): Brave

Colm (M): Dove, peace

Conan (M): Great, wisdom

Conor (M): Desire; wise; hound keeper. One of the most famous

Irishmen of legend was King Conor. Also spelled Connor.

Coyle (M): Leader in battle Dallas (F): Wise

Dolan (M): Dark haired

Emer (F): The beautiful, intelligent wife of the hero CuChulain Erin (F): The name actually means "female" in Irish Gaelic.

Ethne (F): Sweet kernel of a nut - strong on the outside, tender in. Fergus (M): Strong

Galvin (M): Sparrow

Jilleen (F): Youthful

Keeley (M): Handsome

Keelin (F): Fair, slender

Keena (F): Brave

Kevin (M): Handsome

Liam (M): Protector

Maeve (F): Goddess of Song. One of the most famous

Irishwomen of legend was Queen Maeve.

Maureen (F): Great one

Myrna (F): Beloved Niall (M): Champion Patrick (M): Noble

Regan (M): Royal

Rori (F): Brilliant

Ronan (M): Pledge, promise

Shannon (F): Wise

Sheila (F): Musical

Thomas (M): A twin

Costume and Dress

The Irish were very practical people and often clothes would be passed along from family member to family member, being tucked in and adjusted along the way to accommodate wear and size differences.

Outfits for both genders would be rugged and able to survive rough handling. Most families did not have enough money for "special" clothes - they would simply try to keep one set cleaner than most for wearing to church and other occasions. They would often have one good sweater, heavy and thick, to wear over the shirt of the day.

On the other hand, an Irish person might have a treasured brooch, ring, or other item which was of the finest quality. For example, here is an enameled brooch which Bob's mother bought for me in Ireland.

Irish Movies

For such a small island, it's amazing how many films have been made in or about Ireland. The land seems to capture the heart and the imagination. Ireland is a place of stories and story tellers. Here is a collection of stories you can share with those you love.

Angela's Ashes, 2000

Adapted from the multi-award-winning novel by Frank McCourt, this story tells of a young boy growing up in the dirty streets of Limerick.

Agnes Browne, 2000

Starring Angelica Houston (and directed by her as well), this tells the story of a newly widowed Irish woman in the late 60s who tries to raise her seven kids on her own. A bit clichéd and lighthearted, but a fun tale of women helping each other out.

Braveheart, 1994

Sure, this movie wasn't *about* Ireland, but parts of it were certainly filmed there! The plains of the Curragh of Kildare was where the 13th century Battle of Stirling was set. Trim Castle was filmed to represent (from different angles) both the York and London castles. I have to note that this came out at the *same* time *Highlander* did, so when we went to see it in the theater we kept being tempted to yell out "Heather!!"

The Boxer, 1997

With 'Some Mother's Son', this closes the Jim Sheridan trilogy about the IRA. Some Mother's Son isn't really directed by Jim Sheridan, but he is the producer and writer of the film. Daniel Day-Lewis and Emily Watson also star in The Boxer.

Bronte, 1983

Julie Harris stars as Charlotte Bronte, recreating the great author's life.

Broth of a Boy, 1959

This comedy starring Barry Fitzgerald tells of a TV executive trying to do a story of the world's oldest man.

Cal, 1984

A widowed librarian and a young man have a passionate love affair amidst the violent background of the conflict long afflicting the city of Ulster. The film score was composed by Mark Knopfler of Dire Straits.

Captain Lightfoot, 1955

Rock Hudson and Barbara Rush star in this tale of the 19th century Irish rebellion.

Catholics, 1973

Martin Sheen is sent to try to tug an Irish monastery out of their 'backward' ways. The Irish, of course, dig in their heels.

Circle of Friends, 1995

Three young women grow up in a small village (Inistioge, County Kilkenny) and end up going to Trinity in Dublin together. The gorgeous one sets her sights on a local noble, the orphan on a friend, but the 'wallflower', Benny, goes after the most handsome boy on campus. Love and betrayal follow. Set in 1949, this has many nice shots of Dublin, Trinity, and the lands around Kilkenny.

The Commitments, 1991

Directed by Alan Parker, the movie has Colm Meaney (as all good Irish films do) as the father of the 'manager' of a soul band in Dublin. While striving for musical bliss, the members of the band fight, swear, have affairs with each other and walk through streets where children play in broken glass. A stunning statement of the true strength of will of the Irish. While I did like it a lot, it depressed me how all the adults constantly swore in anger at the children. What a way to grow up.

The Closer You Get (a.k.a. American Women)

Starring Ian Hart, some Irish guys from a small village place an ad in a Miami newspaper, asking for American women to come.

The Count of Monte Cristo, 2002

Richard Harris and Luis Guzman are only two of the great cast members in this one which, while not quite faithful to the famous book by Alexandre Dumas, still tells a good tale. Most of the movie is filmed in Malta, but the Count's huge castle is located in Ireland and other sets were built in Ireland as well.

The Crying Game, 1992

Steven Rea, Forest Whitaker, Miranda Richardson. An IRA kidnapping goes wrong, and one of the men goes into London to find the hostage's lover. Briefly in Ireland at the beginning of the movie, but with an Irish-related theme. Interesting plot twists keep this one going.

Da, 1988

Martin Sheen, a writer, returns to Ireland for his father's funeral, and ends up discussing the good and bad of life with his father's ghost, his mother's ghost, 'himself as a child', and even his dog's ghost. In the end, he understands his father better than he had before. It takes place on the coast near Dublin - Dun Laoghaire and Bray - and has scenes from his parent's youth (1900s), his own youth (1920s), and his middle age (1950s). A 'landmark' *grin* - this seems to be the first movie with a fatherless child in the story. This seems to be tradition in Irish film which takes off in a few years, as you'll read further along in the list.

Dancing At Lughnasa, 1988.

Meryl Streep stars as one of five female children in a 1936 rural Irish village. The girls are all unmarried and are trying to cope with their lives and with the changes in society.

Danny Boy, 1984

An Irishman sees a double-murder and tromps across county Armagh to hunt the killer. From the director of the Crying Game.

Darby O'Gill and the Little People, 1959

Sean Connery and Janet Munroe star in this movie about a boastful caretaker who accidentally runs into a group of leprechauns and tricks them into giving him three wishes.

The Dead, 1988

A poignant movie adapted from the James Joyce story by John Huston, this is a tale of a group of friends and family who love music, getting together to celebrate. There are lots of "personalities" - the responsible man, the elderly singer, the pro- independence, zesty young woman. Most funny of all is Colm Meaney appearing in the middle!! He must be in every recent Irish movie. Anjelica Houston is the female lead. The "gaunt house" is located on Usher's Island in the River Liffey.

December Bride, 1993

Another 'bastard child' story? Who would have thought it in an Irish movie! A young Irish woman in a rural area is tired of life with her religious, widowed mother. She falls for the two brothers they work for, and decides to be with them both. The town is scandalized when she refuses to marry either (or, of course "Name the Father"), and rears the child 'without a surname'. She is disgusted that the minister wants to have her marry just to 'give a smooth surface to everything, even though the insides are botched'. A very good telling; the rough sea and land in Northern Ireland are beautiful.

The Devil's Own, 1997

Brad Pitt and Harrison Ford star in this movie about a young IRA terrorist who is taken in by an unknowing New York policeman. A drama about the choices people make in life.

Disco Pigs, 2001

Two children are born at the same time in a Dublin Hospital. The girls, known as Pig and Runt, form an incredibly strong bond that is at once comforting and also restricting.

Divorcing Jack, 1998

A dark comedy about the coming of peace to Northern Island after decades of strife.

Educating Rita, 1983

This is listed as a 'comedy about an English housewife who tries to learn with the drunken College Professor tutor, Michael Caine, tutoring her'. Indeed, the 'blond bimbo' has an English accent (a rough one), while Caine is the cultured but inebriated teacher who often teaches sloshed. It is a truly well done story, a 'tragedy' in the true sense of the word. However, the whole time we're watching it we're thinking, Ireland? There were no Irish accents. No "Irish" scenery, nothing noticeable about the town. All shots in the school and in the 'dirty streets' are incredibly generic. At the end, though, it admits to being shot entirely in Ireland! The college was (of course) Trinity College in Dublin, and the 20s cafe was 'Dobbins Wine Bistro'.

The Englishman Who Went Up a Hill and Came Down a Mountain , 1995

Hugh Grant, Colm Meaney. A cartographer is convinced by local inhabitants that their perception of their land is correct. Actually filmed in Ffynnon Garw, Wales, but the film does feature Colm Meaney.

Excalibur, 1981

This movie is not about Ireland, but was filmed in Ireland because of the great medieval forests which still grow there. This is a retelling of the classic Arthurian legends, done in an earthy and rich way. It has Patrick Stewart as Guenevere's father, and Nigel Terry (from The Lion in Winter) as Arthur. Directed by John Boorman. Unknown to many, the "English" movie was mostly shot in Wicklow. They filmed at Childers Wood, one of the few remaining medieval oak forests in Europe, and Wicklow Head.

The Fantasist, 1986

Christopher Cazenove stars in this movie about a psychotic killer who lures his victims over the phone. His latest victim is a country woman in Dublin.

Far and Away, 1991

Starring Tom Cruise and Nicole Kidman, a typical 'strive against all odds' romance story. The young farmer and his landlord's daughter start out in a small village in Kerry (looks like it's near Dingle). They both run away, sailing to America to gain some land. The Left Bank of Dublin at Temple Bar was transformed into 19th Century Boston, where they live amidst other Irish immigrants and get both support and degradation from them. Eventually they get out to the great land run in the midwest. Only a small portion of the movie takes place in Ireland, but you get a good glimpse of the difference between a small village and the life of the landlords. It's also interesting to hear again of the 'importance of the land', and to see how Irish treated their own in a day when the Irish were looked down upon by other Americans. Of course, the most amusing part is the appearance of Colm Meaney; it seems either he or a Colm-lookalike is in every Irish movie we see.

The Field, 1991

Directed by Jim Sheridan, this story has Richard Harris as a stubborn farmer fighting to keep his land from "The American", Tom Berringer. The farmer's son is played by Sean Bean, who became famous playing Boromir in Lord of the Rings. Adapted from a play, there is a lot of interpersonal drama - nobody is 'good' or 'bad'. It contains a lot of comment on the famine. It's set in dark hills by the water: Leenane in the northwest of Galway, at the head of Killary Harbour. Even the homes are gritty and earthy. A true classic.

The Fighting O'Flynn, 1949

Douglas Fairbanks Jr. is a young gallant lad helping to fight off Napoleon's attack in the 1800s. Note: While this is the "back cover info", I've also been told that the Irish begged Napoleon for assistance in kicking the English out, so that actually to prevent him coming in was preventing an ally of Ireland from coming to rescue them. Everything has a bias!

Finnegan's Wake, 1965

This Joyce classic is well done; a Dublin man envisions his own wake and how it would progress.

Four Days in July, 1984

This comedy has two couples (one Protestant, one Catholic) who meet in a Belfast maternity ward. Quite a funny movie.

Frankie Starlight, 1995

Gabriel Byrne, Matt Dillon. A dwarf grows up in Ireland in love with astronomy, and lives a life confused by love, his mother's loves, and life.

Gangs of New York, 2002

It's not really an Irish film, but all the characters are Irish, so you can consider it. Starring Daniel Day-Lewis, Leonardo Di Caprio, Liam Neeson, the tale focusses on the conflicts in New York City in the late 1800s. Irish men were being shipped off to the Civil War daily. The "native Irish" were resentful of the incoming "immigrant Irish" who were fleeing the effects of the famine. The tensions led to riots.

The General

Directed by John Boorman, and starring Brendan Gleeson, this is the story about a man murdered by the IRA.

The Girl with Green Eyes, 1964

An innocent Irish girl (Rita Tushingham) arrives in Dublin and falls for a cold, older man (Peter Finch). Adapted from the best-selling Edna O'Brien novel.

Harry's Game

A TV movie about the IRA and terrorism, with a famous title song by Clannad.

Hidden Agenda, 1990

An American activist and British policeman team up to investigate a brutal police incident in the 1980s.

The Informer, 1935

Director: John Ford. This film received high marks from many film reviewers. It tells of Gypo Nolan, a heavy drinker, who turns in his friend in order to get a reward during the Irish Rebellion in 1922. The movie is based on the novel by Liam O'Flaherty. McLaglen won an Oscar as best actor; Ford as best director, writers for best screenplay.

In the Name of the Father, 1994

This movie, starring Daniel Day-Lewis and Emma Thompson, is extremely well done. It tells of a young thief who annoys the IRA by causing trouble and stirring up the occupying troops. He is sent out of Northern Ireland by his 'da' to England. There, he is falsely accused of an IRA bombing, and he and his father struggle for justice. Based on a true story (The Guildford Four). There are also scenes shot in Dublin, using Georgian Merrion Square and the Kilmainham Jail. Directed by Jim Sheridan.

Into the West, 1993

Gabriel Byrne in a story of two kids running off with a prize racehorse into the west of Ireland.

Juno and the Paycock, 1930

Directed by Alfred Hitchcock. A tragic tale of an Irish family coping with unrest in Dublin.

The Lonely Passion of Judith Hearne, 1988

Maggie Smiths shines as a lonely spinster who wiles away her years because of a misunderstanding.

The Love She Sought, 1990

Angela Lansbury is a retired schoolteacher who travels to Ireland to meet her pen-pal. She discovers all is not what it had seemed.

The Magdalene Sisters, 2003

One of the sad truths about Ireland is that it was (and is) very restrictive of its females. Women who were thought to be 'too pretty' or who were raped were sent off to 'laundries' to repent for their sins. Stigmatized and sentenced to a life of hard labor, even those who escaped rarely told of the life there.

Man of Aran: 1934

A documentary of life on the Irish island of Aran.

The Matchmaker, 1997

This great love story stars Janeane Garofalo as an American who is sent to the fictitious town of Ballinagra for her political boss. She ends up in the middle of a matchmaking festival and great fun. It was actually filmed in Roundstone, in County Galway.

Michael Collins, 1996

A true story of the 1920s and '30s, set in Dublin and Radthrum, county Wicklow. This political tale stars Liam Neeson as Michael Collins, Alan Rickman as the IRA leader, and Julia Roberts as Michael's love interest. Michael is in charge of 'mayhem' as Liam tries to talk and ineptly fight the war. Michael does a much better job at guerilla tactics, especially when Liam is off 'negotiating' things. The movie seems to be an anti-English movie, and also strangely enough an anti-IRA movie. The IRA is seen as 'doing what they had to do' until the English grant them statehood, but then the 'good guys' try to work with that statehood while the 'evil guys' keep dissenting, insisting on getting Northern Ireland too.

The Miracle, 1991

Beverly D'Angelo goes to a small Irish village where a lonely teenage boy falls for her.

Miller's Crossing, 1990

Gabriel Byrne, Albert Finney. Violent gangster film set in the 30s.

The Molly Maguires, 1970

Richard Harris, Sean Connery. This movie isn't in Ireland at all, but is about Irish coal workers in pitiful conditions in Pennsylvania in the 1870s. Kids and adults are sent into the ground for long, grueling hours, breathing in coal dust under a candle in their hat. They're docked for all the supplies they use - axes, explosives, everything. They barely survive on their meager income. Strikes had failed, so now a small group is blowing up caves to make their point. Connery is in charge of these "Molly Maguires", while Harris is an undercover agent sent in to ferret them out. Very slow movie, but poignant look at how the Irish had to live.

My Left Foot, 1989

Academy award winner Daniel Day-Lewis is Irish poet Christy Brown who overcame cerebral palsy to become a famous writer. It's a poignant tale - while Christy is growing up, everybody thinks he's unintelligent because he can't communicate at all. Only his mother has faith in him - his father's an abusive drinker. Finally one day he writes "MOTHER" with his foot and they realize he *is* intelligent. He begins to paint, and has a showing, but still the girls tease him and he's lonely. He falls in love with his caregiver and is hurt when she marries someone else. A touching story of overcoming difficulties.

The Nephew, 1988

A young man, half black and half Irish, comes to Ireland to bury his mother. He finds out the reason his mother left for the US. He falls in love with a young Irish woman but their families disapprove. Starring Donal McCann, Pierce Brosnan, Sinead Cusack and Hill Harper. Directed by Eugene Brady.

Odd Man Out, 1947

James Mason stars in this classic film noir directed by Carol Reed. An Irish rebel, being hunted by police in Belfast, encounters both friend and foe in his flight. Well done drama, one of the first to address "The Troubles" between northern and southern Ireland.

The Outsider, 1979

An Irish-American heads back to Ireland to help out the IRA, but discovers he's being used as a tool for propaganda instead.

Paddy, 1970

Milo O'Shea stars in a movie about a Dublin youth who escapes harassment at home in an entertaining way.

Parnell, 1937

Clark Gable stars in this tale of the man and how his political career was ruined. Good historical movie - a must for someone looking to understand recent Irish history.

Patriot Games, 1992

Harrison Ford, Patrick Bergin. Not really in Ireland (except for a brief scene or two). An ex-CIA man accidentally aborts an IRA splinter group hit and is targeted by them for the rest of the movie.

Pigs, 1984

Squatters trying to share an area of Dublin have their lives revealed in an exceptional manner.

The Playboys, 1992

Aidan Quinn, Albert Finney and Robin Wright star in this tale filmed in County Cavan, and set in 1957. Oh, let's see. It has ... a woman with a bastard child! She won't "Name the Father"! A carnival comes to town and she falls for one of the gypsies and considers running off with him too! A classic blend of all of the standard Irish stories we keep seeing. Was Colm Meaney in here somewhere? A subtle tale - watch for the many dead-on acting jobs by these actors and actresses, who portray well what life in a quiet Irish village was like.

A Portrait of the Artist as a Young Man, 1979

The classic James Joyce coming of age story tells of Stephen growing up in the early 1900s and his struggles with faith. Directed by Joseph Strick.

A Quiet Day in Belfast, 1984

Starring Barry Foster and Margot Kidder, the drama has twin Irish Catholic girls in Northern Ireland. One of the twins falls for a British soldier.

The Quiet Man, 1952

John Wayne as Sean Thornton, and Maureen O'Hara as Mary Kate. The movie was filmed in Cong, between Lough Corrib and Lough Mask (between Mayo and Galway). Ashford Castle, seen in some shots, is on the shores of Lough Corrib. Mary tended her sheep on what is now their golf course! The horse race (much unlike any other I'd seen!) was at Tully Strand on Connemara, and Thornton's cottage still stands at Teernakill in Maam Valley. The movie won two Oscars, one for cinematography. A must see, it's quite funny (stereotypical) in its portrayal of Irish folk.

The Rise of the Moon, 1957

Irish drama. Famed Abbey players perform three Irish short stories.

Riverdance

Okay, not really a movie, but a must see! This, and *any* video of the Chieftains or the Clancy Brothers are great fun.

The Run of the Country, 1995

Set in the lovely quiet of County Cavan (just south of the North Ireland border), a police offer deals with his son after the wife's death. The son is 18 and falls in love, while the father wants him to go to NY. Interesting tale.

Ryan's Daughter, 1970

Starring Robert Mitchum and Sarah Miles, this story of love and passion was directed by David Lean. It's a long tale about a young woman growing up, and choosing between a solid schoolmaster and an energetic young English soldier. Being Northern Ireland, few villagers approve of the English. Unlike most of the other movies in this list, the people are harsh and cruel, teasing the local cripple mercilessly. The father, Ryan, appears loving and loyal but has secrets of his own. The town is rough and dirty, the ocean incredibly powerful and destructive. It was filmed mainly on the Dingle peninsula in Kerry (not *quite* Northern Ireland). The village of "Kirrary" was actually an area behind the village of Carhoo in Dunquin. Only a street and the famous schoolhouse remain.

The Secret of Roan Inish, 1994

Filmed amongst the beautiful islands of Rosbeg and Portnoo, County Donegal (on the western coast). The story has a young girl, Fiona, sent back to live with her grandparents while the rest of the family moves to the 'city'. Her grandparents and young cousin love the ocean. Her youngest brother was taken by the seals when he was a baby; Fiona gets to know the seals and gulls and asks for him back.

Song O' My Heart: 1929.

This musical stars John McCormack and Alice Joyce. It tells of an Irishman who looks after the orphaned children of the woman who broke his heart.

Shake Hands with the Devil, 1959

James Cagney is a medical professor who also secretly helps run the IRA of the 1920s. He's only for a Republic of Ireland, and fights his own friends when they wish to sign the treaty. A young medical student, whose father was killed in the Hall of Records, first refuses to join the fight. He is swept into it, and ends up playing a pivotal role. Like Michael Collins 40 years later, it shows both the English and the hard-liner Irish to be "bad" and the middle-of-the- road Irish to be "good". Everyone suffers, though. Good movie.

The Snapper, 1993

The classic "Irish" movie - Colm Meaney and a fatherless child. Colm is the father of six children in a grimy Dublin suburb, squashed into a tiny house which itself is squashed in with other houses in a row. The oldest daughter, 19, is pregnant and refuses to name the father (in Irish movie tradition). She continues to go out drinking every night with friends, dancing at bars until the bitter end. Good 'real life' view of the common life in Dublin, even if the scenes of a pregnant woman drinking heavily, Colm swearing at the children (another Irish movie tradition?), and especially the lack of 'judgment against' the 'father' are disturbing.

Some Mother's Son

With 'The Boxer', this closes the Jim Sheridan trilogy about the IRA. Some Mother's Son isn't really directed by Jim Sheridan, but he is the producer and writer of the film. Daniel Day-Lewis and Emily Watson also star in The Boxer.

This is My Father, 1999

Starring James Caan and Aidan Quinn, this movie tells of a middle-aged schoolteacher who heads back to Ireland to track down his father.

Top O' The Morning, 1949

Yet another 'Hollywood'y movie, this one has Bing Crosby searching for the Blarney Stone. As if anyone has to search for it.

The Van

If you like Colm Meany (who, by the way, has a cameo in *Die Hard II* as a plane pilot), you must see this film. It also closes Roddy Doyle's "Barrytown Trilogy", composed of The Commitments, The Snapper, and The Van.

Veronica Guerin

Cate Blanchett of Lord of the Rings fame takes on the real life story of reporter Veronica Guerin who was slain for her work in uncovering drug rings in Ireland. Colin Farrell has a cameo.

Waking Ned Devine, 1998

A funny movie set in the Aran islands but apparently shot on the Isle of Man. Someone in the town has won the lottery, but it's difficult to sort out just who!

War of the Buttons, 1984

The children of a 'scruffy' village are always at odds with the uniform-wearing boys of the nearby town. It all starts when the townies call the villagers 'tosspots'. Unsure of what the term actually means, the villagers are still upset and sneak over to paint messages on the townie's church. Who steps out of the store but .... Colm Meaney! Yes, we got quite a laugh. He's ever-present. The 'war' escalates between the boys, with them taking buttons as war-trophies. The children, in so many ways, are merely emulating the adults of their towns without realizing it. It all takes place in West Cork.

Widow's Peak, 1994

Mia Farrow stars in this romantic mystery set in the 20s in Kilshannon, co. Limerick. She's a shy local woman, in love with the dentist, who takes exception to a beautiful American/English woman who moves into one of the large houses on the peak. The comparisons between the elegant homes of the rich and the 'rest of the town' are interesting, as is the 'boat race'. Another 'crisp and clean' version of Irish life, extremely interesting plot. Colm Meaney lookalike near the end, and yes, a fatherless child.

Zardoz, 1973

This bizarre sci-fi futuristic story stars Sean Connory. The plot is unique. Directed by John Boorman, the movie was set in Wicklow (compare this futuristic use of the county against when it was used in Excalibur). You are treated to the purple mountains of Luggala, Sally Gap and the lakelands around Lough Tay and Lough Dan. And, of course, the floating head. A cult classic.

Visiting Ireland

Ireland is, of course, gorgeous. There's no doubt about it. From its misty mountains to its rocky shores, every corner of it shines with beauty.

Here are just a few places you'll want to see on your visit.

Galway

One of the first places that couples think of when visiting Ireland is Galway Bay. It's the birthplace of the Claddagh ring, that eternal symbol of Irish love and faithfulness. It has the gorgeous ocean to one side and to the other are beautiful lakes which hold some of the best fishing in the world. It has a robust arts scene, many shops to visit, and many pubs where music plays into the night.

Be sure to visit Lynch's Castle, which was built in 1490. There are docks where legend tells of Christopher Columbus visiting before his trip to America. There's also the St. Nicholas Collegiate Church which dates from 1320.

Blarney and the Blarney Stone

Who hasn't heard of the Blarney Stone! This famous stone dates back to Queen Elizabeth I, who was trying to force the Irish leaders to accept her as their ruler. Cormac Teige McCarthy, who was the ruler in Blarney, managed to word all of his responses so that he was extremely polite, but that he never accepted her as his ruler. She was very impressed and said he had the gift!

Visitors who wish to achieve this same talent are invited to walk up to the top of the Blarney Castle, and then must hang upside down to kiss the stone.

There are many other attractions near the castle. There is The Rock Close, with the remains of a prehistoric druidic site. There are many gardens and an arboretum as well.

Kildare

One of the most intriguing spots in Ireland is in County Kildare - the Japanese Gardens.

One thing to note about the gardens, and indeed about all of Ireland, is that the Irish expect you to take care of yourself. There aren't giant fences next to cliffs, and you can climb all around ruins. The paths at this garden can be steep and uneven, and you're expected to watch where you walk.

The gardens are laid out like the "life of man", starting with the birth in a cave. You begin the walk of childhood through the "tunnel of ignorance" (a pitch dark tunnel) and then emerge into the light. After adolescence there is a decision path - choosing bachelorhood instead of marriage and childhood. Each walker can choose for himself or herself whether to move along to the island of engagement and marriage bliss. Both move along to an area of disappointment, then head up to 'the hill of achievement'. After that comes wisdom, and the enjoyment of life. There's even a teahouse to enjoy in the center of the garden.

The gardens are right near the National Stud, where you can learn about the history of horses in Ireland. You can also walk through the stables and fields where the horses are grazing and enjoying the fresh air. This is especially great in the late spring, when the young foals are out!

Dublin

Dublin is a modern, cosmopolitan city which also has many ancient structures worth visiting. It has something for everyone, and is quite fast paced. There are coffee shops, movie theaters, and art galleries alongside national treasures and historic cathedrals.

Dublin is split by the River Liffey, and has stood on this location for over a thousand years. There is St. Stephen's Green with all of its history, Temple Bar with its cafes. Genealogists will find a wealth of knowledge in the archives here. The National Gallery, Trinity College, and many other museums can be found in the city. The Book of Kells is a great treasure - every day a new page is put on display.

Waterford

Waterford is the ultimate destination spot for someone craving culture and quiet. There is everything from ancient historic sites to gorgeous gardens to exquisite craftsmanship.

First, there are the historical sites. There is the Molana Abbey, the Waterford Castle, and the Knockboy Ogham Stones.

There are countless gardens maintained here. The Curraghmore Estate has been the home of the Marquis of Waterford since the 1100's. The Lismore Castle features a garden with an Elizabethan design. Also be sure to visit the Mount Congreve Gardens and the Dromana House and Gardens.

Waterford is, of course, best known for its Waterford Crystal. The visitor center is open most days from 9am to 5pm, and you can watch the master craftsmen create their crystal masterpieces, and admire some of their best work in the museum.

Giant's Causeway

Located on the northern coast of Ireland, the Giant's Causeway is the result of lava heating and cooling over many years. It has turned the basalt lava into an amazing set of 'hexagonal columns' pressed up against each other. From the top, all you see is a series of hexagonal blocks, seemingly forming a pathway out into the ocean.

Ancient Celts were amazed by this formation. They felt it was created by Finn McCool, a giant Ulster warrior who commanded the armies for the King of Ireland. Apparently Finn fell in love with a lady giant off in the Hebrides, and he built this pathway so that she could come home with him.

Nearby is the Carrick-a-rede, a rope bridge that goes out to a small island. It's a swinging bridge and spans an 80 foot drop.

Further along the coast is Bushmills, home to the Bushmills distillery. This is the oldest legal distillery in Ireland, and deserves a visit!

Cliffs of Moher

Many visitors enjoy the rugged western coastline, with its castles and gorgeous views. One of the most photographed views in Ireland is the Cliffs of Moher. This snaking cliff-line is extremely steep and is home to many sea birds, including puffins.

Note that there are cliff walks along the cliffs which literally have you jumping over gaps in the path. Many American tourists let their children play along the edge, figuring that if it were dangerous it would be fenced off with barbed wire. The cliffs in fact ARE dangerous and should be treated with respect.

The beauty of these cliffs is legendary and well worth a visit!

Glossary of Irish Terms

A Chara: A friendly opening in a letter, sort of like an English letter beginning "Dear Mary". It means "friend" in Irish Gaelic.

Aran: Small islands to the west of Ireland, famous for their thick fisherman's sweaters. Each family created its own design so sweaters could easily be told apart. Note that the fable about them being used to identify the bodies of their drowned fishermen seems to be a modern invention. Still, they're pretty!

Banshee: A ghostly figure who usually foretold a death.

Besom: A short brush used for sweeping ashes from the hearth.

Blarney: From the Blarney Stone, the Gift of Gab. The legend of the Blarney Stone is that any who kiss it will become eloquent and persuasive.

Bodhran: a small hand drum made of wood and goat skin.

Bog: swampy land from which blocks of peat are cut to heat homes.

Book of Kells: A gorgeous manuscript done in the 800s by Irish monks, full of "illumination", or colored images.

Bundling: The practice of wrapping a man and woman separately in bedclothes, then allowing them to spend the night talking with each other with their honor intact.

Cead Mile Failte: One Hundred Thousand Welcomes. Pronounced "Kayd Meela Falltcha".

Cisean: An Irish basket, used for anything from organizing supplies to carrying food. Pronounced "cish-awn."

Claenain: A man who cannot be trusted - a reason that could be given for a woman refusing to marry him.

Claddagh: a ring style created in Galway, indicating that a woman was spoken for.

Coibche: bride-price, paid if the groom was very poor and was marrying up in rank.

Colleen: a generic name for any lass.

Connemara Marble: Sometimes called the "Green Gold of Connemara", this county has marble in light green, dark green, white, and sepia. It is often used in jewelry.

Connemara Pony: A breed of small horse that is bred both to carry children and small adults. Its history traces to the 6th century.

Culchie: country bumpkin, used by those from Dublin.

Curragh: traditional fishing boat used for centuries in Ireland.

Craic: Having fun. Pronounced "Crack."

Eire: The name for Ireland in Irish Gaelic. Pronounced "AY-reh."

Faeries: beautiful mystical creatures who are forever young and who try to steal away celebrating Irish folk to live with them in their misty lands.

Famine: Also "The Famine", the great potato famine of 1846-1850 which dropped Ireland's population from 8 million to 5 million via death and emigration.

Feis: An Irish dancing competition. Pronounced "Fesh."

Fiddle: The classic instrument for any Irish gathering, a fiddle could start the place dancing and keep them going until dawn.

Football: What the US calls "soccer", the Irish call Football. The Irish are great fans of football and have both local and national teams.

Gaelic (Irish Gaelic): The native language still spoken in parts of Ireland. Also known as Irish or Gaeilge

Gaol: love.

Garda: The Irish police.

Guinness: Created in 1759 by Arthur Guinness, this rich beer is practically the national drink of Ireland.

Hornpipe: An Irish style of dance, done in 2/4 or 4/4 time. It uses hard shoes and is often called a sailor's dance. It was once exclusively danced by males.

Hurling: Called the fastest game in the world, hurling is much like field hockey. It is a high-pitched game that requires great skill.

Irish Draught Horse: A stolid horse just over 15 hands high, bred for heavy farm work and cart pulling.

Irish News: Daily paper put out in Belfast, Northern Ireland.

Jackeen: A classy city-dweller, used by city dwellers to describe themselves.

Jig: An Irish style of dance, done in either 6/8 time or 9/8 time. This dance is done in soft shoes and is predominantly done by women.

Leprechaun: A short, mischievous male creature who was said to protect a pot of faerie gold.

Mead: A traditional drink made by fermenting honey.

Mighty: An adjective meaning something is greatly approved of. "This day is mighty fine".

Orange / Orange Order: Those in Northern Ireland (the top 6 counties) who do not wish to become part of a unified Ireland (with the other 26 counties).

Peat: A layer of bog which is cut and dried. It is burnt in stoves to heat homes.

Poteen: moonshine, homemade alcohol.

Public House: What the Irish call a pub.

Reel: An Irish style of dance, done in 2/4 or 4/4 time. Originally from Scotland, the Irish developed the reel with both male and female dancers. This is a very energetic dance.

Rugby: A cross between football and soccer, rugby is much loved in Ireland and has been practiced since at least 1854. The 50 senior clubs of Rugby are followed avidly.

Seanachies: poet-singer historians who would travel with the court of a great lord.

Seisiùn: Irish musicians getting together for fun. Pronounced "Seshoon."

Shamrock: A green, three-leafed clover, used by St. Patrick to explain the concept of the Holy Trinity to the native Irish. Often considered the national symbol of Ireland.

Shillelagh: A stout walking stick used by the Irish to get to and from their destinations.

Shingerleens: Lace, embroidery and small jewelry items on the wedding dress.

Slainte: a toast to health.

Slan: Irish Gaelic for Goodbye. Pronounced "Slawn."

Sliotar: A hurling-ball, used in the traditional Irish game of hurling.

Soft: A misty, lightly rainy day.

Tinker: A wandering vagrant, both romantic and looked-down-on for their rootlessness.

Uisce Beatha: Whiskey (i.e. Water of Life in Irish Gaelic)

Uilleann Bagpipes: Irish pipes which are meant for the pub and dancing music, as compared to Scottish bagpipes which were created for war songs.

Yeats, William Butler: An Irish poet who won the Nobel Prize for Literature in 1923.

Web Resources

The web is a fantastic source of information on Ireland, from its history and culture to travel information and current news. Here are a few places to check out.

General Information

BellaOnline Irish Culture
http://irishculture.bellaonline.com/
The Irish Culture editor reviews things to see and do in Ireland.

Government of Ireland
http://www.irlgov.ie/
The Irish Government's website leads you to information on organizations, departments, and travel in and around Ireland.

Ireland.com
http://www.ireland.com
Information on where to go, what to see, and a background to understand the culture.

News

The Belfast Telegraph
http://www.belfasttelegraph.co.uk/
News from Northern Ireland, with world news as well.

The Irish Examiner
http://www.examiner.ie/
A wealth of interesting articles.

The Irish Independent
http://www.unison.ie/irish_independent/
Full on line information from the Irish Independent.

The Irish Times
http://www.irishtimes.com
Run by the Irish Times, the key newspaper in Ireland, this site has
up to date news as well as background and history on Ireland.

Travel

Aer Lingus
http://www.aerlingus.com/
This airline is the main method for entry and exit from Ireland.
Get fare quotes and other customer care information on their
website.

Blarney Castle Website
http://www.blarneycastle.ie/
Visit the castle, kiss the stone, and get the gift of gab.

GenUKI Genealogy
http://www.genuki.org.uk/
A fantastic source for genealogical information about Ireland and
nearby islands.

Discover Ireland
http://www.discoverireland.ie
Run by the National Tourism Service of Ireland, this site is a great
reference for anyone planning a trip to the Emerald Isle.

StayInIreland
http://www.stayinireland.com/
This website helps you find bed & breakfasts, inns or other lodging
in various parts of Ireland.

Trinity College - Book of Kells
http://www.tcd.ie/Library/bookofkells/
This is Trinity College's site about the Book of Kells. It contains a
history of the book, plus images and more.

Music and Traditions

The Chieftains
http://www.thechieftains.com/
One of the best known Irish bands plays both traditional and contemporary music.

Corpus of Electronic Texts (CELT)
http://www.ucc.ie/celt/
These online resources let you read through historical Irish documents on line.

Irish and Scottish Poetry
http://suburbanbanshee.net/irishptr/
Maureen O'Brien has translated many old Irish and Scottish poems on a large number of topics. This is where you can find her many works.

Irish Traditional Music Archive
http://www.itma.ie/
Both in English and Irish Gaelic, this website discusses the great archives held of Irish Music in Dublin.

Riverdance
http://www.riverdance.com/
This dancing sensation has performed in just about every part of the globe. Find out when they will be coming near you.

Valkryie Music
http://valkyriepub.tripod.com
Harp music, both traditional and new. Shirley has a wide selection of harp music available. One of her harp songs might be perfect to become "your song"!

Merchants

Achill Knitwear
http://www.achillknitwear.com/
Quality Aran Irish sweaters and clothing.

Belleek Pottery
http://www.belleek.ie/
Fine Irish china and porcelain in a number of styles.

Guinness
http://www.guinness.com/
The classic beer of Ireland has its own website with history and memorabilia.

Murphy of Ireland
http://www.murphyofireland.com/
Founded in 1939, this classic Irish store stocks everything from jackets to linens, sweaters and much more.

Simply Irish
http://www.simplyirish.com/
A selection of linens, jewelry, marble, and other things Irish.

Waterford Crystal
http://www.waterford.com
The site for Waterford Crystal offers a lot of information on this Irish crystal artistry.

Dedication

This book is dedicated to my mother in law, Barbara Tucker. Barbara might have been born in New York, but she had an authentically Irish heart. She married an Irishman, Tom Tucker from Millstreet, County Cork, and owned a home there.

Barbara became a beloved neighbor on the streets of Millstreet and knew every shopkeeper and passer-by. She lived in her Millstreet home every moment she could. Even when she was in New York, Barbara stayed involved in Irish causes. She was the secretary of the St. Patrick's Day Parade in Yonkers, New York, for over twenty years.

When Barbara died unexpectedly in 2001, two funerals were held, one in Yonkers, New York, and one in Millstreet, Ireland. She was laid to rest on a green hill overlooking her Irish home.

Barbara, we all miss you dearly. We know that you are watching over your Irish town from a joyful part of Heaven, with harps playing and Irish music filling your world.

I wish to thank these individuals who made Weddings and Courtships: Ireland possible:

Jody Zolli, Jenn Mottram, Maureen O'Brien, Shirley Starke, Bob See, and Debi Gardiner.

About the Author

Lisa Shea loves spending time in Ireland visiting with family and friends. Every corner of Ireland offers a new delight. There are the adorable lambs and sheep of Cork who wander the roads with content abandon. There is the incredible scenery of the Giant's Causeway in the north, with its hexagonal rock formations stretching into the sea. The Cliffs of Moher offer great glimpses of puffins with their rainbow-striped beaks.

Best of all, though, are the warm hearts and friendly welcomes of the Irish people. Every pub Lisa visits, every friend she runs into, has her instantly feeling like she was "home." There is always a pint of beer, a friendly game of darts, and a long evening of music and song waiting.

Lisa has been writing about romance since her school days. It was inevitable that her first full book on romantic traditions focuses on the green Celtic delights of Ireland.

The Wedding & Courtships series:

Weddings & Courtships: Ireland

http://www.weddingsandcourtships.com/ireland/

Weddings & Courtships: France

http://www.weddingsandcourtships.com/france/

Weddings & Courtships: Italy

http://www.weddingsandcourtships.com/italy/

Medieval romance novels:
Knowing Yourself
Seeking the Truth
Finding Peace
A Sense of Duty
Creating Memories
Looking Back
Badge of Honor
Lady in Red
Believing your Eyes
Trusting in Faith
Sworn Loyalty
In A Glance

Cozy romance murder mystery series:
Aspen Allegations | Birch Blackguards | Cedar Conundrums

Blackstone Valley mystery novelette series:
Rumble Strip

Sci-fi adventure romance series:
Aquarian Awakenings | Betelgeuse Beguiling | Centauri Chaos | Draconis Discord

Dystopian journey series:
Into the Wasteland | He Who Was Living | Broken Images

Scottish regency time-travel series:
One Scottish Lass | A Time Apart | A Circle in Time

1800s Tennessee black / Native American series:
Across the River | In the Pines

Sci-fi and Massachusetts short stories:
Chartreuse | The Angst of Change | BAAC | Melting | Armsby

Black Cat short stories:
The Lucky Cat – Black Cat Vol. 1

Here are a few of Lisa's self-help books:

Yoga for Stress Relief and Forgiveness
Step by step guidance to improving your health and serenity

Journaling Basics – Journal Writing for Beginners
Everything you need to know to get started with journaling

Quick No-Cook Low Carb Recipes
Heathy, easy recipes with low sugar

Secrets to Falling Asleep
Get better sleep to improve health and reduce stress

Dream Symbol Encyclopedia
Interpretation and meaning of dream symbols

Lucid Dreaming Guide
Foster creativity in a lucid dream state

Learning to say NO – and YES! To your Dream
Protect your goals while gently helping others succeed

Reduce Stress Instantly
Practical relaxation tips you can use right now for instant stress relief

Time Management Course
Learn to end procrastination, increase productivity, and reduce stress

Simple Ways to Make the World Better for Everyone
Every day we wake up is a day to take a fresh path, to help a friend, and to improve our lives.

"Be the change you wish to see in the world."